I0166623

1

This book belongs to:

_____

Cancer Daily Horoscope 2025

Author's Note: Time set to Coordinated Universal Time Zone (UT±0)

Copyright © 2023 by Crystal Sky

Mystic Cat
Suite 41906, 3/2237 Gold Coast HWY
Mermaid Beach, Queensland, 4218
Australia
islandauthor@hotmail.com

All rights reserved. This book or any portion thereof may not be copied or used in any manner without the publisher's express written permission except for using brief quotations in a book review.

The information accessible from this book is for informational purposes only. No statement within is a promise of benefits. There is no guarantee of any results.

Images are under license from Shutterstock, Dreamstime, Canva, or Depositphotos.

Contents

January   16

February   29

March   41

April   54

May   66

June   79

July   92

August   105

September   118

October   130

November   143

December   156

The 12 Zodiac Star Signs

2025

January
S	M	T	W	T	F	S
			1	2	3	4
5	6	7	8	9	10	11
12	13	14	15	16	17	18
19	20	21	22	23	24	25
26	27	28	29	30	31	

February
S	M	T	W	T	F	S
						1
2	3	4	5	6	7	8
9	10	11	12	13	14	15
16	17	18	19	20	21	22
23	24	25	26	27	28	

March
S	M	T	W	T	F	S
						1
2	3	4	5	6	7	8
9	10	11	12	13	14	15
16	17	18	19	20	21	22
23	24	25	26	27	28	29
30	31					

April
S	M	T	W	T	F	S
		1	2	3	4	5
6	7	8	9	10	11	12
13	14	15	16	17	18	19
20	21	22	23	24	25	26
27	28	29	30			

May
S	M	T	W	T	F	S
				1	2	3
4	5	6	7	8	9	10
11	12	13	14	15	16	17
18	19	20	21	22	23	24
25	26	27	28	29	30	31

June
S	M	T	W	T	F	S
1	2	3	4	5	6	7
8	9	10	11	12	13	14
15	16	17	18	19	20	21
22	23	24	25	26	27	28
29	30					

July
S	M	T	W	T	F	S
		1	2	3	4	5
6	7	8	9	10	11	12
13	14	15	16	17	18	19
20	21	22	23	24	25	26
27	28	29	30	31		

August
S	M	T	W	T	F	S
					1	2
3	4	5	6	7	8	9
10	11	12	13	14	15	16
17	18	19	20	21	22	23
24	25	26	27	28	29	30
31						

September
S	M	T	W	T	F	S
	1	2	3	4	5	6
7	8	9	10	11	12	13
14	15	16	17	18	19	20
21	22	23	24	25	26	27
28	29	30				

October
S	M	T	W	T	F	S
			1	2	3	4
5	6	7	8	9	10	11
12	13	14	15	16	17	18
19	20	21	22	23	24	25
26	27	28	29	30	31	

November
S	M	T	W	T	F	S
						1
2	3	4	5	6	7	8
9	10	11	12	13	14	15
16	17	18	19	20	21	22
23	24	25	26	27	28	29
30						

December
S	M	T	W	T	F	S
	1	2	3	4	5	6
7	8	9	10	11	12	13
14	15	16	17	18	19	20
21	22	23	24	25	26	27
28	29	30	31			

2025

Daily Horoscope

CANCER

As your astrologer, I wish to explain why one horoscope book may differ from another for each zodiac sign. The vast array of astrological activity constantly occurring in the sky requires me to focus on the essential aspect of the star sign I am writing for on any given day. Each zodiac sign is unique, and the various planetary factors affect them differently.

When crafting horoscopes, I pay special attention to the significant astrological aspects directly impacting a specific sign. By doing so, I can provide the most insightful and relevant guidance to individuals of that zodiac sign. While there might be multiple planetary alignments on a particular day, one aspect may hold more significance for a specific sign than others.

Considering the ruling planets and elements associated with each zodiac sign further refines my interpretations. This attention to detail ensures that the horoscope resonates with the distinct characteristics and tendencies of the star sign in question.

Ultimately, I aim to offer personalized insights and advice based on each zodiac sign's unique cosmic influences. By focusing on each star sign's most relevant astrological aspects, I can help readers better understand themselves and navigate the energies surrounding them. Embracing each zodiac sign's strengths, challenges, and opportunities allows me to create a horoscope book tailored to my readers' needs.

"We are born at a given moment, in a given place, and, like vintage years of wine, we have the qualities of the year and the season of which we are born. Astrology does not lay claim to anything more."

—Carl Jung

January

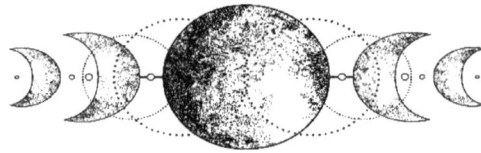

MOON MAGIC

Sun	Mon	Tue	Wed	Thu	Fri	Sat
			1	2	3	4
5	6	7	8	9	10	11
12	13	14	15	16	17	18
19	20	21	22	23	24	25
26	27	28	29	30	31	

New Moon

WOLF MOON

30 Monday

With the Moon in Capricorn and the energy of a New Moon, you may feel a strong sense of determination and ambition. You may focus on practical matters and take a disciplined approach to achieving your objectives. It's a good time for planning, organizing, and taking calculated steps toward aspirations. Embracing a structured mindset and harnessing your inner drive will help you progress. Use this time to set clear intentions and work diligently towards desired outcomes.

31 Tuesday

As the wheel turns full circle, you can take stock of all you have achieved. As you head towards a winning chapter that opens your life with refreshing potential, things move in your social life. It propels you to circulate with friends and engage in an active and lively time shared with valued companions. Surprise news lights the path ahead with an invitation to attend an event. It brings a happy trail that rules a time of expansion and growth.

1 Wednesday

On New Year's Day, with the Moon ingress Aquarius, you may feel a sense of liberation and innovation in the air. This celestial alignment encourages you to embrace uniqueness and think outside the box. It's a time to connect with like-minded individuals and foster community. Embrace the forward-thinking energy of the Aquarius Moon and allow it to inspire you to break free from old patterns and embrace a fresh perspective.

2 Thursday

Bunkering down and formulating a plan brings improvement as you map out a trajectory offering stellar growth. You generate luck and expansion through your willingness to work on your life. Focusing on a pioneering path takes you closer to realizing your dreams. Setting intentions brings key avenues into focus. Planting the seeds for future growth enables life to blossom under sunny skies. Something new and exciting emerges to tempt you forward.

3 Friday

As Venus enters Pisces, you may experience a deepening of emotions. This transit encourages you to connect with your heart. It's a time to explore your artistic side, allowing your imagination to soar and your dreams to take shape. As the Moon enters Pisces, your intuition and sensitivity heighten, enabling you to tap into the spiritual realm and find solace in introspection and self-care practices. Embrace the nurturing energy and find peace in connecting with your inner world.

4 Saturday

With the Sun sextile Saturn, it encourages you to take practical steps toward achieving your long-term goals and aspirations. It's a time to make solid plans, set realistic expectations, and diligently work towards your objectives. You possess the determination and perseverance to overcome obstacles and establish a solid foundation for success. This alignment supports your ability to prioritize and focus on what truly matters, allowing you to make steady progress and gain recognition.

5 Sunday

As the Moon enters Aries, you may feel energy and enthusiasm coursing through your veins. This fiery and dynamic lunar placement ignites your inner drive and propels you forward with courage and assertiveness. You are motivated to take the initiative and pursue your goals boldly and fearlessly. Your emotions may be more impulsive and spontaneous during this time, urging you to embrace new beginnings and tackle challenges head-on.

6 Monday

The square between Mercury and Neptune may introduce a bit of confusion and illusion into your thought processes. It's essential to be cautious of misinformation or misunderstandings that can arise during this time. Double-check facts and be mindful of your communication, as there may be a tendency for misinterpretation. Find a balance between your intuition and logical thinking to navigate through any foggy situations that may arise.

7 Tuesday

With the Moon entering Taurus, you may experience a shift towards seeking stability, comfort, and pleasure in your life. You can take the opportunity to indulge in activities that bring you a sense of serenity and contentment, whether enjoying good food, spending time in nature, or pampering yourself. The Taurus energy encourages you to slow down, savor the present moment, and cultivate a deeper connection with your physical senses.

8 Wednesday

With Mercury entering Capricorn, you can expect a shift in your thinking and communication style. You may find yourself more inclined to think strategically and make calculated decisions. Your style becomes more concise as you aim to convey your ideas clearly and succinctly. It's an excellent time to engage in detailed work, research, or activities requiring careful analysis and attention. Harness this energy to set goals and make plans with confidence and authority.

9 Thursday

You're entering a phase where you'll nurture your dreams and aspirations while shedding emotional barriers hindering your progress. This period offers a healing and therapeutic environment that helps you let go of what keeps you from happiness. It's a time when you'll gain a broader perspective on your potential by exploring unique life possibilities. As you cultivate your dreams, long-term goals start taking shape.

10 Friday

With the Moon ingress Gemini, your mind becomes more agile, and you may find it easier to express your thoughts and emotions verbally—favorable for learning, gathering information, and engaging in social activities that stimulate your mind. Emotional well-being links to mental stimulation and social interaction, so be open to new experiences, engage in meaningful conversations, and embrace Gemini's intellectual and communicative energy.

11 Saturday

With a winning chapter in sight, your social life is abuzz with activity, guiding you to connect with friends and engage in active and lively interactions with cherished companions. Surprising news lights up your path with invitations to attend events, introducing you to a happy and expansive phase. As you broaden your horizons, you experience a quick uptick of potential. A fresh cycle begins in your life, removing outdated elements and nurturing renewal and rejuvenation.

12 Sunday

With Mars trine Neptune, your actions offer compassion and idealism. You may feel inspired to channel your energy into creative pursuits or spiritual practices that align with your values. This aspect brings a harmonious blend of assertiveness and sensitivity, allowing you to assert with grace and pursue your dreams with a compassionate and empathetic approach. You can tap into your intuition and trust your instincts, guiding you toward opportunities for growth and fulfillment.

13 Monday

With the Sun forming a trine with Uranus and a Full Moon illuminating the sky, you enter a period of transformative energy. The Sun trine Uranus aspect brings a sense of liberation, innovation, and self-expression to your life. You are encouraged to embrace your uniqueness and allow your authentic self to shine brightly. This aspect sparks a desire for change, freedom, and a break from routine. You feel inspired to explore new ideas and step outside your comfort zone.

14 Tuesday

As the Moon enters Leo and Venus forms a square with Jupiter, you enter a dynamic and vibrant phase in which your emotions and relationships take center stage. The Moon in Leo ignites a sense of passion, self-expression, and creativity within you, urging you to embrace your inner fire and shine brightly. Meanwhile, the square between Venus and Jupiter brings a mix of expansion and tension in your relationships and personal values.

15 Wednesday

A currency of information flows into your life, providing news and options that empower you to make informed decisions. This information ushers in a journey that surpasses the past, opening your life to new experiences that touch every facet. It highlights remarkable opportunities for future growth and expanding life outwardly. This phase offers a chance to deepen your knowledge and expertise, inspiring change and evolution in your life.

16 Thursday

The Sun-opposed Mars aspect brings a strong surge of energy and a desire to take action, but it can also fuel impatience and conflicts. You might feel a push-pull between your ambitions and the need to balance your daily routines and responsibilities. The Moon's ingress into Virgo adds a touch of practicality and a focus on detail-oriented tasks. It encourages you to analyze and organize your thoughts and actions.

17 Friday

With the Sun sextile Neptune, your imagination is alive and vibrant, allowing you to dream big and envision new possibilities. This aspect encourages you to trust your instincts and follow your inner guidance, as it can lead you to profound insights and a deeper understanding. It is a time to indulge in creative pursuits, explore mystical or spiritual practices, and seek moments of solace and reflection. Embrace the gentle flow of this aspect and allow it to guide greater compassion.

18 Saturday

Shifting gears and remaining open to new possibilities and people lead to a connected time, offering pathways for networking. Joint projects with other kindred spirits help you grow and advance your abilities, reaching a broader audience and leading to exciting possibilities. This period marks a brighter, lighter time and dynamic connections with people who promote kinship and harmony, creating a soul-affirming and enriching environment.

19 Sunday

With the Moon's ingress into Libra, your emotional focus turns toward creating harmony and balance in your interactions with others. You seek fairness and cooperation, and relationships take center stage. Additionally, Mercury sextile Saturn enhances your ability to communicate effectively and thoughtfully. It's when you can rely on your disciplined mind and attention to detail to bring practical solutions and productive discussions.

20 Monday

A shift on the horizon brings fundamental changes to your social life. It opens your world to new companions, offering liberation in your life. It illuminates pathways of personal growth, helping you remove any restrictive boxes that may currently limit your life's potential. A new approach draws rejuvenation and renewal, leading you toward a lively crew of unique companions who nurture and support your world.

21 Tuesday

With the Sun conjunct with Pluto, you may experience a deep sense of personal transformation and empowerment. This aspect brings intense energy and the potential for profound self-discovery and empowerment. It encourages you to dive into the depths of your being, facing your fears and uncovering hidden aspects of yourself. The Moon's ingress into Scorpio further intensifies your emotional landscape, inviting you to explore your innermost desires and emotions.

22 Wednesday

Creativity is flourishing, bringing fresh inspiration to your life. You'll make significant strides toward your goals, leading to greater freedom and expansion. Remarkable changes on the horizon allow you to pursue your vision for future growth. You're entering a productive and dynamic chapter that promises progress and good fortune in various aspects of your life. New opportunities enrich your journey, helping you build a strong foundation for the future.

23 Thursday

Mercury trine Uranus brings a harmonious alignment between your thoughts and innovative ideas. It enhances your ability to think outside the box, fostering unique insights and intellectual breakthroughs. This aspect encourages you to embrace unconventional approaches and embrace individuality. Today offers a blend of dynamic energy, assertiveness, and intellectual agility. It's time to embrace change, think creatively, and take inspired actions to pursue your goals.

24 Friday

With the Moon's ingress into Sagittarius, you may embrace a spirit of adventure and exploration. This aspect ignites a desire for freedom and expansion, urging you to seek new experiences and broaden your horizons. You feel renewed optimism and enthusiasm, eager to embark on unique physical and mental journeys. Your curiosity heightens, and you may desire to learn about different cultures and philosophies or study subjects.

25 Saturday

This alignment of Venus and Mars ignites a spark of creativity and drive within you, inspiring you to pursue your passions with enthusiasm and confidence. It is a time of alignment between your desires and actions, allowing you to experience a sense of fulfillment and joy in your relationships and endeavors. Embrace this harmonious energy and use it to manifest your desires and cultivate meaningful connections.

26 Sunday

With the Moon ingress Capricorn, you enter a period of grounded emotions and practicality. Your focus shifts towards long-term goals and responsibilities as you become more disciplined and determined in your approach. This lunar influence encourages you to set clear intentions and work diligently towards achieving them. Meanwhile, Mercury sextile Neptune brings a touch of inspiration and heightened intuition to your communication style.

27 Monday

Your priorities are shifting in a way that fosters growth, advancement, and productivity. Your dedication to these priorities helps create an environment of well-being and happiness. Embracing a fresh outlook, you'll receive information that unveils the key to prospects and helps elevate your emotional well-being to new heights. Confidence is growing as you connect with inspiring opportunities that encourage your growth.

28 Tuesday

As the Moon ingresses Aquarius, your emotions align with your intellectual pursuits. You may experience a heightened sense of detachment and objectivity, allowing you to approach your feelings with a rational mindset. This lunar placement encourages you to explore your emotional world through the lens of logic and reason. It's a time to embrace your individuality and unique quirks as you connect with individuals who appreciate your unconventional nature.

29 Wednesday

With Mercury conjunct Pluto, you enter a phase of intense mental focus and deep insights. Your thoughts delve into the depths of your subconscious, uncovering hidden truths and unearthing powerful revelations. This aspect empowers you to penetrate beyond the surface and get to the heart of matters, enabling you to perceive the underlying dynamics and motivations. Your communication style becomes persuasive as you express your ideas with conviction and authority.

30 Thursday

The Sun's trine to Jupiter amplifies the positive energy surrounding you. This harmonious aspect brings your life a sense of expansion, abundance, and optimism. It encourages you to embrace growth opportunities and have faith in your abilities. You may feel a renewed sense of purpose and confidence, allowing you to take bold steps toward your goals. It is a time to explore new horizons, broaden your perspectives, and believe in the possibilities.

FEBRUARY

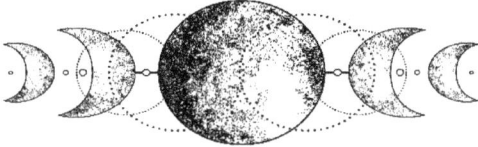

MOON MAGIC

Sun	Mon	Tue	Wed	Thu	Fri	Sat
						1
2	3	4	5	6	7	8
9	10	11	12	13	14	15
16	17	18	19	20	21	22
23	24	25	26	27	28	

New Moon

Snow Moon

31 Friday

Perseverance draws a heartening result as improvement looms overhead, bringing a sunny vista. A new chapter highlights more stability flowing into your life. You'll connect with pathways that offer social engagement and rising possibilities for your love life. You'll discover a climate ripe with blessings and happiness, a bond deepening with someone who inspires your mind and brings fresh energy into your life.

1 Saturday

When Venus aligns with Neptune, it casts a magical and dreamy spell over your relationships and creative endeavors. You may find yourself drawn to romantic and ethereal experiences, seeking deeper connections that transcend the material realm. This cosmic union encourages you to tap into your imagination and express emotions through artistic pursuits. It's a time to explore the beauty of love, compassion, and spiritual connections.

2 Sunday

Moon ingress Aries. You feel a strong need for independence and the courage to assert yourself in various areas of your life. It's a time to embrace new beginnings, set clear intentions, and fearlessly pursue your goals. Trust your instincts and be proactive in taking the necessary steps to manifest your dreams. Allow the Moon in Aries to fuel your determination and propel you toward personal growth and self-discovery.

3 Monday

With Mercury forming a harmonious trine aspect to Jupiter, you get a heightened sense of intellect, optimism, and expansive thinking. You have a natural ability to see the bigger picture and find the silver lining in any situation. It favors learning, studying, and acquiring knowledge, supporting personal and professional growth. Embrace this positive energy and use it to broaden your horizons, seek expansion opportunities, and embrace the abundance that awaits you.

4 Tuesday

As Venus moves into Aries, fiery and passionate energy ignites your desires and prompts you to assert yourself in love, creativity, and personal expression. Meanwhile, Jupiter's direct motion amplifies your optimism and expands your opportunities for growth and expansion. You can now move forward with confidence, trusting in your abilities and the positive outcomes that lie ahead. Allow the harmonious interplay of these cosmic energies to guide you to success.

5 Wednesday

News on the horizon kicks off an exciting chapter, triggering an active phase of goal development as you immerse yourself in the broader world of potential. This cycle of growth blossoms into a meaningful path forward. Connecting with friends brings a sense of optimism and a smoothing of the rough edges in your life. A new approach takes prominence, and rising confidence draws vitality into your surroundings.

6 Thursday

Moon ingress Gemini is a time to embrace intellectual stimulation, expand your knowledge, and seek diverse perspectives. You may find yourself drawn to social gatherings, networking opportunities, or engaging in activities that promote mental stimulation and connection. Embrace the energy of the Gemini Moon as it invites you to embrace the power of communication, curiosity, and mental exploration.

7 Friday

With Venus forming a harmonious sextile aspect to Pluto, you find yourself experiencing deep and transformative connections in your relationships and personal life. This alignment brings intense emotions and a heightened passion and desire. You draw experiences and people that profoundly impact your heart and soul. It's a time of deep self-discovery and the potential for profound healing and growth.

8 Saturday

You may feel a stronger connection to your home and loved ones, craving their presence and support. Trust your intuition, as it brings you a sense of emotional fulfillment. Pay attention to your needs and take the time to nurture yourself and others. Allow the gentle and compassionate energy of Cancer Moon to embrace you, offering a safe space for self-reflection and healing. Take solace in the warmth of home and the loving connections that bring you a sense of belonging.

9 Sunday

With the Sun in conjunction with Mercury, your mind is sharp, and your communication skills heighten. You can express yourself with clarity and conviction, making it an ideal time for meaningful conversations, negotiations, or sharing your ideas. Your thoughts and words carry a powerful impact, and you can effectively convey your intentions and desires. This alignment encourages you to speak your truth and assert your ideas confidently.

10 Monday

As the Moon enters Leo, you step into vibrant and expressive energy. Your emotions heighten, and you're ready to shine and embrace your individuality. This transit is a time for self-confidence, creativity, and passionate self-expression. You radiate warmth and charisma, drawing others towards you with your magnetic presence. Your inner fire ignites, and you're inspired to pursue your passions wholeheartedly.

11 Tuesday

When the Sun squares Uranus, you may experience a sense of restlessness and unpredictability. This aspect brings sudden and unexpected changes that can disrupt your routine and challenge your stability. It encourages you to break free from limitations, embrace individuality, and seek new and unconventional paths. It's a time to embrace spontaneity and be open to unique opportunities that come your way.

12 Wednesday

The Full Moon brings a sense of clarity and awareness, illuminating areas of your life that may need attention or release. Emotions may run high, urging you to acknowledge and process unresolved feelings. It is a powerful opportunity to celebrate achievements, gain insights, and make adjustments in alignment with your authentic self. Take time to honor your journey and embrace this lunar phase's wisdom.

13 Thursday

Moon ingress Virgo. You may feel a heightened sense of responsibility and a desire to serve others. This period offers an opportunity to assess your health and well-being, making adjustments to support your physical and mental wellness. Embracing the energy of the Moon in Virgo, you can channel your attention to the practical aspects of life, bringing a sense of purpose and accomplishment to your daily endeavors.

14 Friday

Mercury ingress Pisces. It's a favorable period for expressing love and affection and engaging in heartfelt conversations. Let your imagination and intuition guide your interactions, allowing for a deeper emotional connection and a sense of enchantment in your relationships. Take the opportunity to express your innermost thoughts and feelings, as the energy of Mercury in Pisces supports open and heartfelt communication.

15 Saturday

As the Moon moves into Libra, you seek harmony and balance in your relationships and surroundings. This transit encourages you to focus on cooperation and diplomacy, valuing the opinions and needs of others. You are naturally inclined to create a peaceful and harmonious atmosphere within your relationships or in your immediate environment. You feel a stronger desire to connect, seeking companionship and social interaction.

16 Sunday

Anticipate refreshing changes on the horizon that inject new energy into your social life, allowing you to reconnect with friends. Exciting news is on the horizon, bringing a refreshing aspect to your social life. Opportunities to mingle are vital to advancing toward greener pastures, ultimately nurturing well-being and harmony in your world. Sharing with your circle of friends reveals new ideas that support your life and guide you toward a brighter destination, fostering outward growth.

17 Monday

Your world begins to shine as you enter a brighter chapter of social growth. New opportunities are on the horizon, expanding your social horizons and pushing you to make exciting plans with others. It lets you enjoy the excellent company of friends and fosters a lively atmosphere. Embracing new friendships brings lively conversations and magical connections that energize and enrich your surroundings.

18 Tuesday

Moon ingress Scorpio, Sun ingress Pisces is when your intuition heightens, and you may feel more connected to the spiritual dimensions. It's a time to tap into your creativity, compassion, and empathy, allowing yourself to flow with the currents of inspiration and understanding. Embrace the depth of your emotions and the power of your intuition as you navigate this phase. Trust in your inner wisdom and explore the realms of your subconscious, for they hold the key to joy.

19 Wednesday

Life is about to bless you with a renewed sense of inspiration. It reinvigorates your creativity and motivates you to tackle your goals head-on. As you embrace your passions and unique skills, doors of opportunity start to open. You'll soon embark on a journey that brings you closer to your vision of future success. The elements align to provide you with solid foundations and positive outcomes in your life. It translates into a more fruitful phase where you can develop your talents.

20 Thursday

As the Moon moves into Sagittarius and Mercury forms a square with Jupiter, you may feel a surge of enthusiasm and a thirst for knowledge and exploration. Sagittarius' influence inspires you to expand your horizons, seek new experiences, and embrace a sense of adventure. You are eager to learn, grow, and broaden your perspective on life. However, the square aspect between Mercury and Jupiter reminds you to approach this journey with caution and discernment.

21 Friday

Fresh options make a grand entrance, breathing new life into your social sphere. This pathway advances your life's journey, and you can trust your instincts to guide you in the right direction. Lighter energy aids in building stable foundations, securing a gratifying outcome. It ushers in a time for networking and mingling with friends, landing you in a supportive environment with heightened social engagement.

22 Saturday

Moon ingress Capricorn. Embrace the qualities of perseverance and self-discipline as you navigate challenges and work towards your aspirations. Capricorn's influence can help you develop a sense of authority and leadership. Take charge of your responsibilities and make decisions that align with your long-term vision. By staying committed and dedicated, you can progress significantly toward your goals and create a solid framework for your future success.

23 Sunday

You're about to discover valuable options worth exploring, uncovering new sources of prosperity. Sharing with friends infuses a lucrative boost of happy energy that enhances harmony. Expanding your social life continues to nourish your spirit, propelling you to achieve your vision for future growth. Concentrating on your goals unveils a significant lifestyle change on the horizon, opening up a unique path forward.

24 Monday

Mars turns direct is a time to channel your inner drive and use it as fuel to propel you toward your desired outcomes. With Mars moving forward, you are encouraged to embrace your courage, initiative, and assertiveness, allowing you to make significant strides in various areas of your life. Trust in your abilities and let this forward motion inspire you to embrace the challenges and opportunities that lie ahead.

25 Tuesday

Moon ingress Aquarius. Mercury conjunct Saturn. Use these cosmic alignments to organize ideas, make strategic plans, and approach challenges logically. The combination of Aquarian lunar energy and the Mercury-Saturn conjunction empowers you to think outside the box and approach problems from a fresh perspective while maintaining a systematic and pragmatic approach. Embrace this cosmic synergy to unlock insights and manifest ideas with clarity and purpose.

26 Wednesday

A sense of excitement and purpose builds as you step into a brighter phase of your journey. There's a clear path ahead that nurtures your talents and provides opportunities for personal growth. You'll soon be exploring new avenues and developing your skills as you work towards achieving your goals. Your life is undergoing positive changes, offering you stability and balance in your career and personal life.

27 Thursday

The sextile between Mercury and Uranus brings innovation and intellectual stimulation to your thoughts and communication. It opens the door for unexpected insights and a willingness to embrace change. You can explore new perspectives and engage in stimulating conversations that broaden your horizons. Embrace the fluidity and imaginative nature of Pisces as you tap into the electric energy of Mercury and Uranus with inspired ideas and breakthroughs.

MARCH

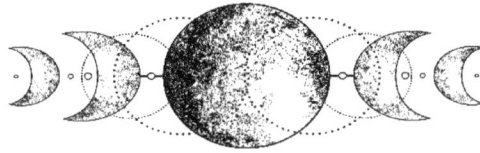

MOON MAGIC

Sun	Mon	Tue	Wed	Thu	Fri	Sat
						1
2	3	4	5	6	7	8
9	10	11	12	13	14	15
16	17	18	19	20	21	22
23	24	25	26	27	28	29
30	31					

NEW MOON

WORM MOON

28 Friday

The New Moon is a time of introspection and self-discovery, where you can connect with your innermost dreams and aspirations. Take this opportunity to tune into your intuition, align your intentions with your values, and take inspired action toward your dreams. As the Moon begins its waxing phase, you can work on manifesting your intentions and witnessing the expansion of your goals. Trust in the power of this fresh lunar cycle and embrace the potential for beginnings.

1 Saturday

The Aries Moon encourages you to step forward confidently and enthusiastically, ready to tackle any challenges. It's a time for boldness, independence, and self-expression. Trust your instincts and be open to new adventures and opportunities. Allow the energy of Aries to fuel your drive and determination, propelling you forward. Embrace the spirit of initiative and embrace the thrill of blazing your trail. This lunar phase allows you to ignite your inner fire and make your mark.

2 Sunday

During Venus retrograde, you may experience a shift in your relationships and how you perceive matters of love and beauty. Reassessment brings a deeper understanding of what truly brings you joy and fulfillment. Mercury conjunct with Neptune, your intuition and imagination heighten, allowing you to tap into your creative flow and access more profound realms of thought. However, the Sun square Jupiter can challenge balancing optimism and practicality.

3 Monday

You may feel a more substantial need for security and a desire to surround yourself with people and experiences that bring you a sense of groundedness and serenity. It's an excellent time to indulge in self-care activities and seek emotional nourishment through life's simple pleasures. Allow the combination of Mercury in Aries and the Moon in Taurus to inspire you to express yourself boldly and seek emotional harmony in your interactions and surroundings.

4 Tuesday

The changes ahead bring a positive aspect, with reward and happiness running rife as new ideas and epiphanies set in motion the development of unique adventures. You take a journey encompassing your dreams and desires as you grow your goals, talents, and skills, shaping your life as you see fit. Making yourself a priority brings good luck and prosperity into your world, ruling a time of expansion that helps you extend your reach and promote a new growth area.

5 Wednesday

Moon ingress Gemini, Mercury sextile Pluto alignments empower you to communicate with depth and influence, captivating others with your words. It's a time of heightened mental clarity and transformative conversations that can bring significant personal growth. Embrace the power of your thoughts and engage in meaningful exchanges that have the potential to shape your understanding of yourself and the world around you.

6 Thursday

Life brings opportunities that offer a new source of prosperity. Refining this potential connects with learning and creativity. It links you with developing a journey that aligns with the person you are becoming as you improve circumstances through a willingness to broaden your horizons. It encourages you to push past limitations and expand your horizons into new areas. Stepping past your comfort zone lets you develop regions that come calling to grow your talents.

7 Friday

With the Moon moving into Cancer, your feelings become more pronounced, and you may seek comfort, security, and familiarity. This transit is a time to nurture yourself and create a safe space to express and process your emotions. Your intuition heightens, and you may feel more vital empathy toward others. It is an opportunity to strengthen your emotional bonds and cultivate a sense of belonging in your relationships and home environment.

8 Saturday

With the Sun forming a harmonious trine aspect to Mars, you reveal a powerful surge of energy and motivation. Your drive and ambition heighten, igniting a sense of confidence and assertiveness within you. This aspect encourages you to take bold action and enthusiastically pursue your goals. You feel a strong sense of determination and vitality, fueling your ability to initiate new projects and overcome challenges.

9 Sunday

Moon ingress Leo transit encourages you to tap into your inner joy and express yourself authentically. You may find yourself seeking activities that bring you pleasure and indulging in self-expression through various forms, such as art, music, or performance. The Leo Moon inspires you to shine brightly and positively impact those around you. It's a time to celebrate your individuality and embrace the opportunities for self-expression that come your way.

10 Monday

Inspiring progress leaves you optimistic as you enter a dynamic environment that enhances your productivity and success, becoming the gateway from which you deepen your knowledge and advance your skills. You plot a course towards developing your skills, ushering in growth and learning, and igniting inspiration as you establish your talents in an exciting direction. It highlights more stability flowing in as you launch towards growth in the career sector.

11 Tuesday

Mercury conjunct Venus heightens your appreciation for art, beauty, and aesthetics, inspiring you to seek creative and pleasurable experiences. You may find yourself drawn to engaging in artistic pursuits or indulging in the finer things in life. Use this harmonious energy to express yourself creatively, share your ideas with others, and foster a greater sense of harmony and beauty in your interactions and surroundings.

12 Wednesday

Moon ingress Virgo and Sun conjunct Saturn alignment emphasize the need for perseverance, hard work, and long-term planning. You may encounter challenges or obstacles but can overcome them with determination and a patient mindset. You can lay a solid foundation for future success by embracing discipline and organization. Focus on the details, prioritize your tasks, and use your practical wisdom to navigate any challenges that come your way.

13 Thursday

News arrives, bringing a lucky break, a surprise emerging out of the blue and filling your life with excitement. It helps you make the most of growing your world outwardly. Being open to new opportunities lights up your life with possibility, with an incoming assignment sparking a busy time and bringing glorious developments around creativity and expression. It rules a time of expansion that helps extend your reach and promote a new growth area.

14 Friday

With the Moon entering Libra, there is a greater emphasis on finding equilibrium and seeking fairness in your interactions. It prompts you to consider the needs and perspectives of others, fostering cooperation and diplomacy. Embrace the transformative energy of the Full Moon, the unexpected opportunities brought by the Sun's sextile with Uranus, and the balancing influence of the Moon in Libra to create more harmony and fulfillment in your life.

15 Saturday

Take this moment to pause, reassess your strategies, and pay attention to the details. Use this Mercury retrograde phase as a chance to tie up loose ends, revisit unfinished projects, and focus on inner reflection. Embrace the slower pace and allow yourself to find hidden gems of wisdom within this temporary backward motion of Mercury. By cultivating patience, mindfulness, and adaptability, you can gracefully navigate this retrograde period and emerge with a fresh perspective.

16 Sunday

It begins with small changes that add up over time, creating an extensive pathway that grows your circle of friends, emphasizing improvement of circumstances, and cultivating lighter energy that breaks up the stagnant patterns currently holding you back from achieving your most authentic path. Removing the blocks that stall progress enables you to get busy developing your world in a refreshing direction, bringing a lively atmosphere of social engagement.

17 Monday

When the Moon ingresses Scorpio, it brings your life intense emotional energy. You may find yourself delving into the depths of your feelings and uncovering hidden truths. This cosmic phase is a time of transformation and regeneration, where you can let go of old patterns and embrace personal growth. Your intuition heightens, allowing you to navigate complex emotional situations with insight and sensitivity.

18 Tuesday

Being open to new possibilities draws a pleasing result, with news arriving that excites you about prospects. It helps you take steps towards developing a long-held dream, making you busy in an environment that kickstarts growth, bringing the perfect time for cooking up a storm of new ideas. Planning is instrumental in making the most of opportunities that cross your path, sealing the deal on rising prospects ahead, and marking a prosperous chapter.

19 Wednesday

Moon ingress Sagittarius. Sun conjunct Neptune. You may find yourself drawn to creative pursuits or spiritual practices that ignite your imagination and connect you with a higher realm of existence. Embrace the sense of wonder and possibility surrounding you, allowing yourself to listen to your intuition and higher wisdom. Align with your spiritual path and trust in the divine flow. Embrace the journey ahead with an open heart and a willingness to explore the depths of your soul.

20 Thursday

Sun ingress Aries. Vernal Equinox. Use this potent energy to set clear intentions, take bold actions, and ignite the spark of inspiration within you. Aries's fiery nature and Equinox's transformative power let you embark on a journey of self-discovery, and you can embrace the opportunities that lie ahead. Trust in your abilities, follow your instincts, and let the vibrant energy of this season propel you forward on your path of personal growth and fulfillment.

21 Friday

When Venus sextiles Pluto, a powerful and transformative energy that infuses your relationships and personal connections, you can deepen your emotional bonds and explore the depths of intimacy with others. This aspect invites you to embrace the transformative power of love, allowing it to bring profound changes to your life. You may find yourself drawn to experiences that evoke passion, desire, and a sense of personal empowerment.

22 Saturday

The Moon in Capricorn encourages you to take a structured and systematic approach to your emotions, allowing you to navigate challenges calmly and composedly. It is a time to embrace your inner strength, perseverance, and determination to overcome any obstacles that come your way. This lunar transit empowers you to make practical decisions, establish solid foundations, and work towards achieving your ambitions.

23 Sunday

When the Sun is conjunct Venus, you can expect a harmonious blend of self-expression and interpersonal connections. This aspect enhances your charm, attractiveness, and ability to form meaningful relationships. You may experience a greater desire for love, beauty, and balance, leading you to seek pleasurable experiences and appreciate the finer things. The Sun sextile Pluto adds depth and transformative energy to the mix, empowering you to make positive changes.

24 Monday

Aquarius, an air sign, focuses on innovation, unconventional thinking, and social consciousness. Your emotions may become more detached and rational, allowing you to approach situations with a logical perspective. It's a time when you may feel inspired to express your unique ideas. The Sun's conjunction with Mercury further enhances your communication skills and mental agility, making it a good time for expressing your thoughts and engaging in intellectual pursuits.

25 Tuesday

When Mercury sextiles Pluto, it brings a powerful blend of mental intensity and depth to your communication and thought processes. This aspect encourages you to delve deep into your thoughts and explore profound subjects with a keen analytical mind. Your ability to uncover hidden truths heightens. This alignment supports research, investigation, and discovery of valuable insights. It empowers you to communicate with depth, persuasion, and influence.

26 Wednesday

Moon ingress Pisces. Allow yourself to explore the mystical and spiritual realms, finding comfort in the intangible aspects of life. Remember to take care of yourself during this sensitive time, creating a peaceful and serene environment that supports your emotional well-being. Trust in the wisdom of your heart and let your intuition guide you toward a deeper understanding of yourself and the world around you.

27 Thursday

When the Black Moon enters Scorpio and Venus moves into Pisces, a potent and mysterious energy envelops your emotional landscape. You may feel an intensified connection to the hidden depths of your psyche and a longing for profound emotional experiences. The combination of Venus and Neptune brings an enchanting and dreamy quality to your relationships and desires. You may draw romantic and spiritual connections that transcend the ordinary.

28 Friday

As the Moon enters Aries, you feel a surge of fiery energy and assertiveness within you. Your passionate and vibrant emotions motivate you to take bold action and embrace new beginnings. You're eager to explore uncharted territories and dive headfirst into exciting endeavors. This lunar ingress ignites your courage and determination, urging you to trust your instincts and pursue your goals with unwavering confidence.

29 Saturday

During the New Moon phase, you can start anew and set powerful intentions for the future. It's a time of fresh beginnings and untapped potential. As the Moon aligns with the Sun, you connect with your innermost desires and envision the life you want to create. This aspect is a fertile moment to plant the seeds of your dreams and aspirations, allowing them to take root and grow. Use this time to reflect on what you genuinely want and consciously decide to manifest it.

30 Sunday

The Moon's ingress into Taurus grounds stabilizes your emotions, providing a sense of inner security and practicality. You are encouraged to indulge in simple pleasures, finding comfort and peace in the present moment. This cosmic dance invites you to embrace the power of your imagination, trust your inner guidance, and anchor your dreams into tangible reality. Allow this harmonious interplay of energies to guide you in manifesting your visions with grace and determination.

APRIL

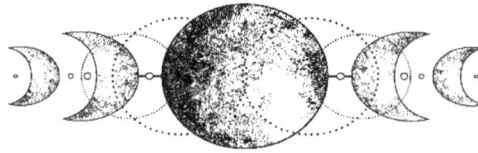

MOON MAGIC

Sun	Mon	Tue	Wed	Thu	Fri	Sat
		1	2	3	4	5
6	7	8	9	10	11	12
13	14	15	16	17	18	19
20	21	22	23	24	25	26
27	28	29	30			

New Moon

PINK MOON

31 Monday

Improvement ahead boosts your confidence, bringing lighter energy into your life and helping you harness creative abilities and develop your skills as you head towards rising possibilities. It takes you towards a prosperous landscape that offers advancement, providing a productive time that nurtures growth and stability. As you improve your bottom line, you continue to branch out and create momentum by being open to new possibilities that tempt you forward.

1 Tuesday

As the Moon enters Gemini, you feel a sense of intellectual curiosity and a desire for mental stimulation. Your mind becomes adaptable and eager to explore new ideas and gather information from various sources. This lunar transit encourages you to engage in meaningful conversations, share your thoughts and opinions, and connect with others intellectually. It is a time to embrace your natural curiosity, indulge in learning, and expand your mental horizons.

2 Wednesday

There may be an influence holding you back from reaching for your dreams. Taking a moment to release any areas that limit progress helps you build stable foundations. You soon realize that things are ready to shift forward in your life, with news arriving and bringing new information to your door, attracting something you have been seeking into your life, and opening to a time that offers many blessings as you progress towards rising prospects.

3 Thursday

As the Moon moves into Cancer, you are more sensitive and attuned to your emotions. Your nurturing instincts emerge, and you feel a deeper connection to your loved ones and home environment. This lunar transit encourages you to create a safe and nurturing space where you can express and honor your feelings. You find comfort in familiar surroundings and seek solace in the company of those you hold dear. It's a time to listen to intuition and honor your emotional needs.

4 Friday

With Saturn sextile Uranus and Mars sextile Uranus, you can bring balance and innovation into your life. You can harmonize the old with the new, combining stability and structure with progressive change. This cosmic alignment encourages you to embrace your unique individuality and break free from any limitations or restrictions that have held you back. It's a time to tap into your inner drive and assert yourself confidently while being mindful of your actions' impact.

5 Saturday

Mars trine Saturn. You can overcome obstacles and face challenges head-on, utilizing your inner strength and resilience. This alignment encourages you to set realistic goals, work diligently, and make steady progress toward your aspirations. You can harness the constructive energy of this aspect to manifest tangible results and achieve long-term success. Trust in your abilities and the power of your will to navigate any hurdles that come your way.

6 Sunday

The Sun's sextile aspect with Jupiter amplifies your optimism and expands your opportunities for growth and success. This alignment brings a sense of abundance and abundance to your life, encouraging you to embrace new possibilities and take calculated risks. It's a good time for personal and professional endeavors, as you're likely to attract positive attention and receive support from others. The Venus-Mars trine enhances your relationships and brings harmony to your interactions.

7 Monday

With Mercury turning direct, you may experience a sense of clarity and forward momentum in your communication and thought processes. This shift can relieve any delays or misunderstandings that may have occurred during Mercury's retrograde phase. You can move confidently and make informed decisions based on a clearer understanding of your circumstances. It's a time to express yourself effectively, share your thoughts and ideas, and engage in productive dialogue.

8 Tuesday

Venus sextile Uranus. Moon ingress Virgo. It's a time to focus on details, organization, and efficiency, bringing a sense of groundedness and practicality to your endeavors. Use this energy to refine your plans, pay attention to the small things, and strive for perfection in your tasks. The combination of Venus sextile Uranus and the Moon in Virgo encourages you to embrace spontaneity and innovation while maintaining a practical and systematic approach.

9 Wednesday

Life heads to an upswing, and you find solutions to run towards growth, finding balance in an ever-changing environment to discover learning and progression pathways, with bright and cheerful energy flowing into your life, harmonizing and balancing your spirit, and fascinating and mesmerizing possibilities ahead, contemplating the path forward with an eye for detail, opening to a busy time that lets you embrace growing your life.

10 Thursday

An opportunity ahead allows you to share your endeavors with a broader audience, developing creative projects. This fortunate trend brings an uptick of potential, giving you the green light to deepen your knowledge and grow your ideas. You embark on a voyage that reshuffles the decks of fate, bringing rising prospects that facilitate advancement, new leads emerging, which have you thinking about the options, a time of developing areas that motivate change.

11 Friday

As the Moon enters Libra, you seek balance and harmony in your relationships and surroundings. Libra's influence encourages you to prioritize diplomacy, cooperation, and fairness in your interactions. You feel attuned to the needs and perspectives of others, fostering a desire to create harmonious connections and resolve conflicts through open dialogue and compromise. This lunar transit invites you to evaluate the dynamics in your relationships and make adjustments.

12 Saturday

A positive trend is ready to burst forth in your life, with lighter overtones that promote well-being and happiness, making life feel soft and breezy as you engage in a social element that is supportive and nurturing, beginning a time of building stability in foundations that stimulate growth in your social world, where news and invitations spark an engaging time ahead. Sharing with friends connects you with a lively time that promotes a thoughtful path forward in your social life.

13 Sunday

Full Moon. Venus turns direct. Moon ingress Scorpio. With the Moon's ingress into Scorpio, you are encouraged to delve into the depths of your emotions and uncover hidden truths. This lunar energy amplifies your intuition and invites you to explore the mysteries of your inner self. Use this powerful combination of celestial influences to embrace transformation, release what no longer serves you, and embrace the potential for profound growth and healing.

14 Monday

Developing your skills and growing your talents link you with positive change, with developments ahead bringing news and potential into your life. The correct option that feels perfect fits your situation crops up, emphasizing the improvement of circumstances, getting a bumper crop of potential to your door. You attract possibilities that let you dip your toes into a new area of interest worth your time. The tone becomes lighter; enthusiasm weaves gently around your circumstance.

15 Tuesday

Things are shifting towards change, offering unique areas of growth and advancement, bringing new possibilities to help you advance toward your dreams. You open a book of chapters that connect with greater happiness in your life, putting you in contact with like-minded people who celebrate your successes and share thoughtful discussions with you. Overall, the landscape expands, encouraging progression.

16 Wednesday

This combination of the Moon in Sagittarius and Mercury in Aries invites you to express yourself boldly and passionately, explore different perspectives, and pursue your passions with a fiery determination. Trust your intuition and allow the cosmic energy to propel you toward growth and discovery. Embrace the opportunities that come your way and embark on exciting new adventures that align with your true desires.

17 Thursday

When Mercury joins forces with Neptune in conjunction, your mind attunes to imagination, intuition, and spirituality. You may daydream, seeking inspiration from the ethereal and mystical realms. Your thoughts and communication take on a poetic and imaginative quality, allowing you to express gracefully and sensitively. This alignment enhances creativity and intuition, enabling you to tap into subtle nuances and deeper meanings in your interactions and experiences.

18 Friday

Moon in Capricorn brings a sense of practicality and ambition to your emotional landscape. You are focused on long-term success and are willing to put in the necessary effort and discipline to achieve your objectives. This alignment encourages you to balance your desires and responsibilities, harnessing your drive and determination to bring tangible results. It is a time for taking charge, making strategic moves, and pursuing your ambitions with unwavering determination.

19 Saturday

Sun ingress Taurus. Mars trine Neptune aspects enhance your creative and spiritual endeavors, infusing them with magic and inspiration. You may find yourself drawn to artistic pursuits or engaging in selfless service to others. Trust in the power of your dreams and harness the energy of Mars and Neptune to manifest them into reality. Embrace Taurus's earthy, nurturing energy, and let your actions reflect your heart's desires as you navigate this harmonious and soulful alignment.

20 Sunday

As Easter Sunday dawns, it brings forth a unique blend of energies to inspire and uplift you. The harmonious sextile between Venus and Uranus sparks excitement and liberation. Unexpected opportunities for connection and growth may arise, inviting you to embrace the exhilaration of self-discovery. Simultaneously, the sextile between Mercury and Pluto enhances your mental prowess and deepens your understanding of hidden truths and transformative insights.

21 Monday

In the current cosmic dance, the Sun squares Mars, creating a dynamic and potentially challenging energy in your life. This alignment may bring about a sense of tension and conflict, urging you to find a balance between your desires and the actions you take. You may feel a strong urge to assert yourself and pursue your goals, but it's essential to be mindful of impulsive or aggressive tendencies. You can channel energy wisely, using drive and determination to overcome obstacles.

22 Tuesday

Pay attention to clues, with opportunity knocking and bringing potential. As you focus on developing unique options, you gain insight into other dreams and aspirations, and a time of adventure ahead fuels your imagination with creative inspiration, allowing you to cross over to a lighter and happier landscape. Prospects are rising, breathing new life into your dreams, clearing blocks, and establishing stable foundations that light a growth path around your life.

23 Wednesday

Moon ingress Pisces. Sun square Pluto. Navigating this period with awareness is essential, recognizing any power dynamics that may arise within yourself or your interactions. Use this opportunity to engage in transformative inner work, releasing what no longer serves you and embracing personal growth. By honoring the depths of your emotions and engaging in self-care practices, you can navigate the transformative energies of this aspect with grace and resilience.

24 Thursday

The more you grow your path, the more you learn to connect with abundance. An area you become involved with develops changes in your world, setting your sights on a lofty goal, giving you a chance to grow your world, and leading to a significant time of discovery and expansion in your life. In this lush and rich landscape, you boost your abilities and head towards advancement, nurturing your skills to feed creativity and heighten the potential possible in your life.

25 Friday

As Venus aligns with Saturn, you may feel a mix of seriousness and responsibility in love, relationships, and personal values. This conjunction encourages you to assess your connections' stability and long-term potential, seeking solid foundations and commitment. Meanwhile, with the Moon moving into Aries, there is an infusion of fiery energy and assertiveness in your emotional sphere. You feel renewed enthusiasm, independence, and a desire to take charge.

26 Saturday

Exploring and developing leads draw an optimistic influence, touching down on sharing time with friends and kindred spirits. A change of pace brings a refreshing environment, and developments bring news and invitations to social gatherings, creating an essential backdrop for getting together with your tribe. Sharing discussions helps make headway towards a progressive time of growth, immersing your energy in a beautiful environment that promotes happiness and harmony.

27 Sunday

Taurus Moon invites you to find comfort and security in the present moment, focusing on practical matters and nurturing your physical and emotional well-being. The New Moon signifies a fresh start and the potential for new beginnings. It's a time to set intentions and embark on a journey of self-discovery. Embrace the Taurean energy of stability, determination, and sensuality as you navigate the transformative powers of the Mars-Pluto opposition.

MAY

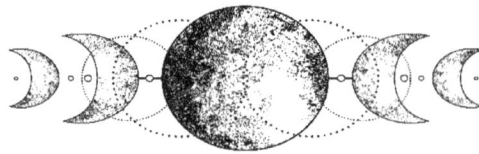

MOON MAGIC

Sun	Mon	Tue	Wed	Thu	Fri	Sat
				1	2	3
4	5	6	7	8	9	10
11	12	13	14	15	16	17
18	19	20	21	22	23	24
25	26	27	28	29	30	31

New Moon

FLOWER MOON

28 Monday

Making informed choices helps you ascertain the correct journey forward for your working life, bringing a time that grows your abilities enabling you to achieve maximum results. Strategy and planning harness the energy of focused intention to place you at a considerable advantage, marking a shift forward that takes your goals to the next level, bringing valuable results and advancement to your career path.

29 Tuesday

Moon ingress Gemini. You may draw diverse subjects and be eager to gather information from various sources. Embrace Gemini's adaptable and versatile nature, allowing yourself to be open-minded and flexible in your interactions and pursuits. This aspect is an excellent time to express yourself, expand your knowledge, and connect with others mentally. Embrace the energy of Gemini and let it inspire your curiosity and desire for connection in all areas of your life.

30 Wednesday

As Venus ingresses into Aries, you may feel a surge of boldness and assertiveness in love and relationships. Your desires and passions ignite, propelling you to take decisive action and pursue what you truly want. Aries brings a fiery and independent energy to your romantic endeavors, urging you to embrace spontaneity and take the lead. This transit encourages you to assert your individuality and express your desires without reservation.

1 Thursday

Moon ingress Cancer. You may find comfort in spending time with loved ones, creating a cozy and inviting atmosphere in your home, and nurturing yourself through self-care practices. Allow yourself to embrace your emotional vulnerability and seek solace in your life's familiar and comforting aspects. This period invites you to cultivate a sense of emotional security and find comfort in the bonds of love and family.

2 Friday

When Venus and Neptune come together, it brings a touch of magic and enchantment to your experiences. You may be more open to the beauty and wonder surrounding you, and your appreciation for art, romance, and spirituality heightens. This celestial alignment encourages you to tap into your imagination and explore dreams and fantasies. You may feel more compassionate, empathetic, and inclined to seek deeper connections with others.

3 Saturday

When the Moon enters Leo, you may feel a surge of confidence and a desire to shine your unique light on the world. This celestial energy encourages you to express your authentic self and embrace individuality. You might find yourself seeking attention and recognition, and there's a natural inclination to take center stage. Let your creative spirit soar and indulge in activities that bring you joy and pleasure. Embrace your inner child and let your playful side come to the forefront.

4 Sunday

Pluto turns retrograde, a time to reassess power dynamics and reclaim your sovereignty. Allow yourself to face fears, confront your shadows, and embrace the transformative energy that Pluto brings. By delving into the depths of your being, you can emerge stronger, wiser, and aligned with your true purpose. Remember that this retrograde is a powerful catalyst for change, and by surrendering to the process, you can embark on a path of profound healing and soul evolution.

MAY

5 Monday

With the Moon's ingress into Virgo, you'll feel a practical and analytical influence, bringing attention to detail and focusing on efficiency. This combination of Mercury sextile Jupiter and the Moon in Virgo creates a perfect environment for problem-solving, organizing, and making practical improvements in your life. You're encouraged to harness the power of your mind, embrace new perspectives, and take reasonable steps toward personal growth and self-improvement.

6 Tuesday

Venus sextile Pluto's a time to embrace the transformative power of love and delve into the depths of your emotions. Trust your instincts and be open to this aspect's transformative potential. Embrace the opportunity to cultivate deeper connections and explore love, desire, and personal transformation. Allow the energy of Venus and Pluto to guide you toward greater intimacy, authenticity, and emotional fulfillment.

7 Wednesday

You discover helpful options, creating a golden triangle of possibility, bringing luck, improvement, and security. Gathering your resources, you are open to a time of learning and refinement that shines on your skills, getting the ball rolling on upgrading your career path and letting you take advantage of incoming opportunities that offer rising prospects. Advancement is coming, bringing a fertile environment to grow your life.

8 Thursday

When the Moon enters Libra, you may seek harmony, balance, and peace in your interactions and relationships. Your focus shifts towards creating a harmonious environment and fostering a sense of fairness and equality. You become more attuned to the needs and perspectives of others, and diplomacy becomes a valuable tool in navigating social situations. You may desire to connect with others intellectually and emotionally, seeking companionship and cooperation.

9 Friday

New options shimmer brilliantly, illuminating your path. In the realm of your social life, a wave of good fortune washes ashore as heartwarming news unfolds. You find yourself mingling with fresh faces, weaving a web of support, and fostering lively conversations. This unique experience uplifts your spirit and provides a soothing balm for your restless energy. Emotions flourish as you transition forward, donning a bright and happy outlook on life.

10 Saturday

As the communication planet Mercury enters Taurus, your thoughts and words take on a grounded and practical tone. You may speak more rationally and focus on factual matters. This transit encourages you to slow down and pay attention to the details, allowing you to express yourself steadily and reliably. At the same time, with the Moon moving into Scorpio, your emotions may deepen, leading to greater intensity and desire for introspection.

11 Sunday

This period teems with lively discussions and stimulating conversations, serving as fertile ground for fostering your creativity. Taking a leap of faith expands your horizons, marking the commencement of a journey that promises a gratifying outcome. Sharing moments adds a delightful touch of excitement and introduces fresh flavors into your social life. It radiates an air of enchantment, dissolving borders and ushering in possibilities that ignite transformative change.

12 Monday

Full Moon. Mercury square Pluto. Use this energy to delve into the depths of your psyche, examining your thought patterns and beliefs. Be aware of power dynamics in your relationships and strive for open and honest communication, even in difficult conversations. This combination of energies invites you to confront and transform limiting beliefs or communication patterns that no longer serve your growth and evolution.

13 Tuesday

As the Moon enters Sagittarius, a spirit of adventure and exploration fills the air. You may feel optimistic and enthusiastic, ready to embark on new experiences and expand your horizons. This transit encourages you to seek knowledge, broaden your perspectives, and embrace the unknown. You may be drawn to philosophical or spiritual pursuits, seeking wisdom and a deeper understanding. It's a time to take bold leaps of faith, trusting that the universe has your back.

14 Wednesday

Good fortune is ready to blossom in your world. Planning and research infuse your creativity with a proactive approach that brings new options to spark momentum. You enter an upbeat and optimistic time of developing goals that offer rising prospects in your world, with a boost to your career path, rekindling motivation and bringing an enterprising time of developing skills, positioning you to progress towards expansion, pushing back the barriers that limit progress.

15 Thursday

Moon ingress Capricorn. The energy of Capricorn invites you to take a mature and disciplined approach to your emotions, allowing you to navigate challenges with resilience and determination. It's a good time for planning, organizing, and setting realistic goals that align with your broader life purpose. Embrace the true nature of Capricorn and trust in your ability to achieve what you set out to accomplish.

16 Friday

Appreciating the upcoming changes, you observe how they sweep away a problematic chapter, allowing you to embark on a transformative journey filled with growth and promising prospects. As you open pathways to abundance, you readily embrace change, shining a light on new life goals. The world around you becomes enriched with possibilities, exuding a palpable sense of optimism. Your journey unfolds toward a lush landscape teeming with fresh possibilities.

17 Saturday

When the Sun aligns with Uranus, you may experience excitement and an urge to break free from the norm. This cosmic alignment can bring unexpected opportunities and sudden changes into your life. You might feel a desire to express your individuality and embrace your uniqueness. This transit is a time to tap into your inner rebel and explore new horizons. You may find yourself craving independence and seeking unconventional paths.

18 Sunday

When Mercury forms a square aspect with Mars, it can create tense and challenging energy in your communication and thought processes. You may feel a strong urge to assert your opinions and defend your ideas, which can lead to conflicts and arguments if not handled with care. Being mindful of your words and reactions during this time is essential, as impulsive or aggressive communication can cause misunderstandings and hurt feelings.

MAY

19 Monday

News arrives, cracking the code to a brighter chapter in your life. You are set to claim a basket of good fortune that promises excellent results, motivating you to enhance your home life and establish sound foundations, ushering in stability and security. Your involvement with a particular area initiates a transformative process, rekindling your vitality as it fuels growing creativity, allowing you to explore new possibilities.

20 Tuesday

When the Sun forms a sextile aspect with Saturn, it brings a harmonious blend of discipline and stability to your life. This planetary aspect encourages you to take practical steps toward your goals and establish a solid foundation for success. You may feel more focused, organized, and determined to achieve your ambitions. It's an excellent time to assess your long-term plans and make necessary adjustments to ensure their realization.

21 Wednesday

Becoming true to yourself puts your goals front and center, marking a prime time for pursuing dreams and soaring towards tremendous success, seeing the more substantial possibilities that bring the drive and resources to get projects off the ground. Focusing on your most pressing desires brings advancement, aligning your actions with your highest good, bringing a progressive time of developing your vision for future growth.

22 Thursday

With the Moon entering Aries, you'll experience energy and enthusiasm. It's a time for taking initiative, asserting yourself, and pursuing your personal goals with courage and determination. You may feel a strong desire for independence and self-expression, and you'll be motivated to tackle any challenges that come your way. This aspect invites you to embrace your passions, tap into your intuition, and fearlessly embark on new adventures.

23 Friday

You enter an exhilarating phase, brimming with activity that breathes new life into your social sphere. The introduction of fresh energy strengthens interpersonal bonds, and a change of pace draws invitations to mingle. This transition allows you to spend quality time with friends and cherished companions. As the wheel of fortune turns in your favor, you'll witness a positive impact on your life. Emphasizing kindling trailblazing discussions illuminates the path to growth.

24 Saturday

With Mercury conjunct with Uranus, your thoughts and communication infuse with brilliance and originality. You may experience flashes of insight and innovative ideas that can lead to breakthroughs in your thinking or problem-solving. This aspect encourages you to embrace your unique perspective and express yourself authentically. It's a time of intellectual stimulation and the potential for exciting discoveries.

25 Sunday

As Saturn moves into Aries, you may feel a shift in the energies around discipline, responsibility, and structure. Saturn's ingress into this fiery sign encourages you to take charge of your ambitions, set clear goals, and establish a solid foundation for your endeavors. Aries brings a sense of initiative and assertiveness, urging you to take decisive action and face challenges head-on. You can adopt a more self-assured and courageous approach to achieving your long-term aspirations.

26 Monday

Mercury ingress Gemini transit enhances your communication skills and intellectual agility, allowing you to engage in lively conversations. With Mercury sextile Saturn, it brings structure and organization to your thoughts and ideas. Your attention to detail and practical approach help you communicate effectively and make sound decisions. As the Moon also enters Gemini, your emotions align with your mental processes, giving you curiosity and a desire for conversations.

27 Tuesday

During the New Moon, a powerful energy of new beginnings and fresh opportunities permeates the air. It's a time of setting intentions, planting seeds, and embarking on transformative journeys. As Mercury forms a trine with Pluto, your mind is sharp and perceptive, able to delve into the depths of your thoughts and uncover hidden truths. This alignment empowers you to communicate with insight, making it an ideal time for research, investigation, and deep introspection.

28 Wednesday

As the Moon moves into Cancer, you may experience heightened emotional sensitivity and nurturing energy. Your intuition becomes more pronounced, guiding you toward creating a safe and comforting environment for yourself and others. This aspect lets you pay attention to emotional needs and prioritize self-care. You have a natural ability to connect deeply with your own emotions and the feelings of those around you, fostering a sense of empathy and understanding.

29 Thursday

Opportunity arrives, with upcoming changes promising an improvement in your circumstances. You'll dive headfirst into a sea of refreshing possibilities, advancing your goals and embracing new challenges that stimulate your growth. This buzz of excitement is just the beginning, sparking learning and inspiring your personal and professional development, redefining the boundaries of what's possible in your working life.

JUNE

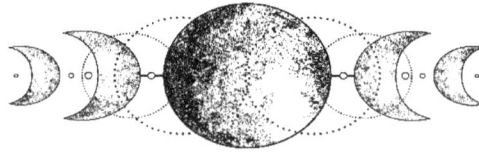

MOON MAGIC

Sun	Mon	Tue	Wed	Thu	Fri	Sat
1	2	3	4	5	6	7
8	9	10	11	12	13	14
15	16	17	18	19	20	21
22	23	24	25	26	27	28
29	30					

New Moon

STRAWBERRY MOON

30 Friday

When the Sun and Mercury align, your mind illuminates, and your communication becomes infused with confidence and clarity. This alignment empowers you to express yourself with authenticity and conviction, making it an excellent time for self-expression and sharing your ideas with others. As the Moon enters Leo, it adds a touch of warmth and creativity to your emotional landscape. You may feel a surge of confidence and a desire to shine.

31 Saturday

You find yourself stepping into a new and exhilarating landscape as significant changes bring expansion and growth. Focusing on building blocks equips you with the tools needed to make the right moves that propel your situation forward. This endeavor sets you on a new adventure that nurtures your inspiration, attracting happiness into your life and connecting you with like-minded people. Social interaction contributes to your well-being and harmony.

1 Sunday

The arrival of curious news provides insights into an engaging and happy time ahead, fostering opportunities for socializing with a broader circle of friends. This phase shines a light on an active and dynamic chapter that aids you in establishing greener pastures in your life. The winds of change introduce fresh possibilities that motivate and inspire you to great lengths. Your willingness to explore unique leads unveils a world of endless possibilities.

2 Monday

As the Moon moves into Virgo, you may find yourself attuned to details and focused on practical matters. Use this time to prioritize your health, establish routines, and tackle tasks precisely and methodically. Embrace the earthy energy of Virgo and harness it to bring order and structure to your surroundings and daily routines. Paying attention to the details and taking care of your responsibilities can create a solid foundation for your personal and professional endeavors.

3 Tuesday

A positive influence becomes the guiding force, allowing you to craft your vision and pursue your dreams. A vast landscape of possibilities tempts you forward, ushering in a progressive and prosperous journey. Life brims with glittering options, fostering social growth and offering positive outcomes. A time of new projects and endeavors is dawning, built on solid foundations, nurturing well-being, and promoting growth.

4 Wednesday

As the Moon moves into Libra, you may notice a shift towards harmony, balance, and a desire for peaceful interactions. You may find yourself more attuned to the needs and perspectives of others, seeking to find common ground and promote cooperation. You may feel a heightened sense of fairness and justice, valuing diplomacy and compromise in your relationships. It's an excellent opportunity to foster harmonious connections, resolving conflicts with grace and tact.

5 Thursday

With Venus sextile Jupiter, you can expect a harmonious and joyful energy to permeate your interactions and experiences. This aspect brings an expansive and optimistic vibe, encouraging you to embrace abundance. It enhances your social connections, promoting enjoyable conversations. You feel confident, making it an excellent time to pursue creative endeavors that bring joy. Additionally, with Mercury sextile Mars, your communication and mental agility heighten.

6 Friday

When Venus ingresses Taurus, it brings a grounding and sensual energy to your relationships and experiences of pleasure. This transit encourages you to embrace the beauty and abundance surrounding you and indulge in simple pleasures. You may find yourself drawn to activities stimulating your senses, such as enjoying good food, engaging in creative endeavors, or surrounding yourself with natural beauty.

7 Saturday

Moon ingress Scorpio transit encourages you to embrace transformation and release any emotional baggage that no longer serves you. It's a period for healing as you process deep-seated emotions. You may also experience passion and desire, seeking intimacy and connection on a profound level. Trust your instincts and dive into the mysterious realm of your emotions. You can uncover insights and inner healing through self-awareness and emotional exploration.

8 Sunday

When Mercury conjuncts Jupiter and ingress into Cancer, it signifies a time of expanded awareness and nurturing communication. You may attract deeper philosophical discussions and seek knowledge that feeds your soul. Your mind is open and receptive to new ideas and perspectives, allowing you to broaden your horizons. This transit encourages you to express thoughts and emotions with empathy and compassion, creating an environment for meaningful connections.

9 Monday

With Venus square Pluto, there may be intense and transformative experiences in your relationships and your connection to your values. This aspect calls for deep reflection, letting go of what no longer serves you, and embracing personal growth. As Jupiter ingresses into Cancer, it brings a sense of emotional expansion and nurturance. You may feel a stronger connection to your home, family, and emotional well-being. You seek emotional security and find meaning in life.

10 Tuesday

Exciting news arrives, heralding a time of excitement and newfound possibilities. As you bid farewell to limitations, you can fully immerse yourself in pursuing your goals. The energy at your disposal allows you to set sail on a new venture, with a productive and engaging environment pushing the boundaries of your world and propelling you forward. Your abilities and talents receive a boost, laying the foundation for personal and professional advancement.

11 Wednesday

Full Moon. Mercury's sextile Venus aspect encourages you to engage in heartfelt conversations and appreciate your interactions' beauty and artistry. It's a reasonable time to express your affections and engage in creative endeavors that bring joy and pleasure. Allow the energy of the Full Moon and the supportive aspect between Mercury and Venus to inspire you to nurture your relationships and communicate from a place of love and harmony.

12 Thursday

Capricorn Moon's influence encourages you to take charge of your life and make steady progress toward your aspirations. This planetary aspect is a time for organization, structure, and taking steps toward building a solid foundation for your future. Embrace the disciplined nature of Capricorn as you set realistic goals and prioritize your commitments. Use this energy to establish a sense of stability and achieve success through your hard work and dedication.

13 Friday

Information arrives, resonating harmoniously with your life. Something significant appears on the horizon, paving the way for rising prospects that expand your world's boundaries. An active and engaging period nurtures thoughtful discussions with like-minded spirits, casting light on an expressive and optimistic environment that promotes companionship. It ushers in a promising chapter of social engagement, promising a delightful outcome.

14 Saturday

When the Moon enters Aquarius, you may experience a shift in your emotional energy towards a more detached and objective perspective. Aquarius is an air sign known for its intellectual and innovative nature. During this time, you may crave mental stimulation and a sense of freedom in your emotions. You may feel drawn to exploring new ideas, connecting with like-minded individuals, and seeking unconventional experiences.

15 Sunday

As Mars squares Uranus and Jupiter squares Saturn, you may experience tension between the need for freedom and the demands of responsibility. Uranus's disruptive energy and Mars's assertiveness can create a strong desire for change. Still, the square aspect of Uranus may bring unexpected challenges and disruptions to your plans—Jupiter's expansive nature clashes with Saturn's restrictive influence, causing a conflict between optimism and practicality.

16 Monday

You may enter a dreamy and intuitive phase when the Moon ingresses Pisces. As a water sign, Pisces encourages emotional depth and a heightened sensitivity to your surroundings. During this time, you may experience increased compassion and empathy towards others and a stronger connection to your own emotions. It's a time to dive deep into your inner world, exploring your subconscious and spiritual realms.

17 Tuesday

When Mars ingresses Virgo, you may experience a shift in your energy and focus. Virgo is an earth sign associated with practicality, attention to detail, and efficiency. With Mars in Virgo, you are encouraged to channel your energy towards organization, productivity, and taking care of the elements in your life. This transit is favorable for tackling projects, setting goals, and implementing practical strategies. You seek to improve routines, health habits, and daily life.

18 Wednesday

When the Moon ingress Aries, you experience a surge of energy, assertiveness, and a desire to take action. Aries is a fiery sign associated with courage, initiative, and a pioneering spirit. During this time, you may feel a sense of urgency and a need for independence. You are motivated to assert yourself and pursue your goals with passion and determination. It's a time to embrace new beginnings, take risks, and trust your instincts.

19 Thursday

When Jupiter squares Neptune, you may find yourself grappling with a sense of confusion or idealism. This aspect can bring about a clash between your aspirations and the reality of the situation. You might feel torn between your desire for expansion and growth and the need to confront the limitations and boundaries in your life. It's essential to remain grounded and realistic during this time, as there may be a tendency to overlook details or be overly optimistic.

20 Friday

Flexibility and understanding become your allies as you navigate through a challenging period, guiding you toward a balanced environment that resonates with harmony and security. Engaging in constructive dialogues seals the deal for a happier chapter, infusing life with positive energy and enabling you to close the door on past problems. Your inner reflections become the catalyst for nurturing your spirit in a unique direction, allowing the way for progress in your life.

21 Saturday

Moon ingress Taurus. Sun ingress Cancer. It is an opportune moment to create a sanctuary for yourself, both physically and emotionally. Take time to indulge in self-care activities, surround yourself with loved ones, and establish a strong foundation for your emotional well-being. The June Solstice adds an extra touch of significance, marking a shift in seasons and an invitation to align yourself with the natural rhythms of life. The nurturing energy guides a fulfilling existence.

22 Sunday

As Mars forms a harmonious sextile with Jupiter, and the Sun engages in a challenging square with Saturn, you find yourself at a dynamic crossroads. The Mars-Jupiter sextile fuels your motivation, ambition, and enthusiasm, giving you the confidence to take bold actions and pursue your goals with gusto. This alignment amplifies your drive and encourages you to step outside your comfort zone, embracing opportunities for growth and expansion.

23 Monday

With the Moon moving into Gemini, you may feel a heightened curiosity and mental agility. This energy encourages you to engage in diverse interests, explore new ideas, and connect with others through open and stimulating conversations. However, be aware of the Sun's square aspect to Neptune, which brings a potential challenge in maintaining focus. This aspect may create confusion or illusions, making it necessary to discern between reality and fantasy.

24 Tuesday

Sun conjunct Jupiter alignment encourages you to embrace a positive mindset and approach challenges with adventure and openness. Your charisma and magnetism attract favorable circumstances and influential people who can support your journey. You can broaden your horizons, gain new knowledge, and make meaningful connections that expand your worldview. Embrace this cosmic alignment, allowing it to inspire you to reach for the stars.

25 Wednesday

With the Moon transitioning into Cancer and the arrival of the New Moon, you are entering a phase of emotional depth and fresh beginnings. This lunar shift invites you to connect with your innermost feelings, nurturing a sense of emotional well-being and security. The New Moon marks a powerful time for setting intentions and planting the seeds of your dreams. It's an opportunity to align your emotions and desires, setting the stage for growth and transformation.

26 Thursday

With Mercury forming a sextile aspect to Uranus and the Sun creating a sextile to Mars, there is an exciting and dynamic energy in the air. This harmonious alignment encourages you to embrace your unique ideas and confidently express yourself. Your mind is sharp and inventive, allowing you to think outside the box and develop innovative solutions. The Sun's sextile to Mars boosts energy and motivation, empowering you to take action and pursue goals.

27 Friday

Allow your passions to guide your goals and dreams. Embrace your creativity and let it flow freely, infusing your life with joy and inspiration. It is a time to celebrate your individuality and express yourself authentically through art, performance, or any form of self-expression that brings you joy. Let your inner radiance illuminate the path ahead and inspire others. Embrace the empowering energy of the Moon in Leo and let it ignite your inner fire.

28 Saturday

Mercury trine Saturn aspect enhances your ability to focus, plan, and organize your thoughts effectively. You feel more disciplined and responsible in your communication, making conveying your ideas and opinions easier with precision and authority. Your attention to detail and practical mindset allows you to tackle complex tasks and challenges. Additionally, the trine between Mercury and Neptune adds a touch of imagination and intuition to your mental faculties.

29 Sunday

In opposition to the planet Pluto aspect, Mercury can challenge your beliefs and push you to question the status quo. It invites you to confront any power dynamics or manipulative tendencies in your interactions with others. While it can be intense, it also offers an opportunity for transformation and growth. The Moon's ingress into Virgo further enhances your analytical and discerning abilities. You are inclined to pay attention to the details and strive for practical solutions.

July

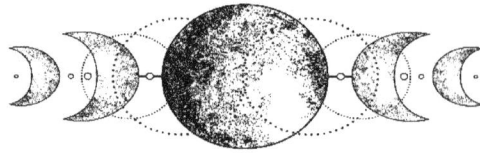

MOON MAGIC

Sun	Mon	Tue	Wed	Thu	Fri	Sat
		1	2	3	4	5
6	7	8	9	10	11	12
13	14	15	16	17	18	19
20	21	22	23	24	25	26
27	28	29	30	31		

CANCER

NEW MOON

BUCK MOON

30 Monday

News of a fresh cycle on the horizon beckons, inspiring growth around your working goals. It empowers you to release old patterns blocking progress. This shift reawakens your awareness of what is possible when you extend your reach and dive into an empowering chapter, increasing your career dreams. Setting goals and creating plans reaps fruitful results, allowing you to tackle high-level assignments that deepen your talents and refine your skills.

1 Tuesday

Moon ingress Libra lunar transit invites you to focus on relationships and connections, valuing cooperation, diplomacy, and fairness. You may feel a heightened awareness of the needs and perspectives of others and a desire to find common ground and mutual understanding. It is a favorable time to engage in social activities, collaborate with others, and find ways to bring more beauty and aesthetics into your life.

2 Wednesday

Being receptive to new opportunities is essential in growing your career path. Momentum gathers, and you redefine your life constructs by being open to advancing your skills to the next level. Working with your abilities attracts a deeper understanding of your natural strengths and skills. It offers a degree of active growth that brings progress into your career path. It takes your abilities to a broader audience ahead.

3 Thursday

Serendipity lights the way ahead, drawing an enterprising journey that offers progress. Advancement comes knocking, and this helps you take the reins and move towards a productive chapter in your working life. It launches your skills into an area that nurtures stability, learning, and growth. Having the correct elements in your life enables you to prosper and thrive. Learning and growth develop your skills and take your talents to the next level.

4 Friday

When the Moon enters Scorpio, you may experience a deepening of emotions and a heightened sense of intensity. This astrological transit invites you to dive into the depths of your feelings and explore the hidden aspects of your psyche. It's a time for introspection and self-reflection as you delve into the mysteries of your inner world. The conjunction of Venus and Uranus brings excitement and unexpected encounters in love and relationships.

5 Saturday

Good fortune flows into your world, adding a touch of excitement and prompting you to dream big about the endless possibilities ahead. This period of spontaneous mingling with friends brings a sense of rejuvenation. A fresh cycle beckons in your life as you share with kindred spirits, invigorating a realm of possibilities. An openness to expanding your world results in pleasing outcomes, offering a time of nurturing social connections and infusing your world with well-being.

6 Sunday

Venus forms a sextile aspect with Saturn, bringing a harmonious blend of stability and creativity into your life. This celestial alignment encourages you to balance your desires for love, beauty, and pleasure and your need for structure, responsibility, and commitment. You may experience an appreciation for the relationships and partnerships that provide joy. With Venus sextile Neptune, there is a touch of magic and inspiration in your romantic and creative endeavors.

7 Monday

As Uranus enters Gemini, it brings a fresh wave of innovative and transformative energy to your life. This transit encourages you to embrace change, think outside the box, and explore new possibilities. It sparks your curiosity and ignites your intellect, inspiring you to seek knowledge and expand your understanding of the world. Meanwhile, Venus forming a trine with Pluto deepens your emotional connections and empowers your transformation.

8 Tuesday

By nurturing the foundations in your life, you cultivate a balanced and stable environment, allowing new leads to emerge and sparking your interest in growth. An opportunity for learning presents itself, serving as a wellspring of inspiration and offering both challenges and opportunities for advancing your career path. An openness to developing your skills moves your life toward greener pastures, ushering in an extended period of growing your dreams.

9 Wednesday

Moon ingress Capricorn. You can tap into your inner resilience and use it to overcome challenges and obstacles that come your way. Take advantage of this lunar influence to establish a solid foundation for your endeavors and steadily progress toward your ambitions. Your practical mindset and the Moon's influence can bring stability and a sense of accomplishment. Embrace the Capricorn energy and let it guide you toward success.

10 Thursday

The energy of the Full Moon encourages you to trust your intuition and follow your heart's desires. Use this time to celebrate your achievements, express gratitude for the abundance in your life, and set intentions for the next phase of your journey. Allow the Full Moon's energy to guide you in finding a sense of wholeness and fulfillment. Embrace this powerful lunar energy and let it illuminate your path forward.

11 Friday

When the Moon enters Aquarius, you may feel a shift in your emotional energy. This transit is a time to embrace your individuality and uniqueness. You may seek intellectual stimulation and connect with like-minded individuals who share your interests and ideals. It's a time to think outside the box and explore new ideas and perspectives. You may feel inspired to contribute to your community or engage in social causes that align with your values.

12 Saturday

New information cracks the code to a brighter chapter, opening the gate to a fresh start that marks the commencement of a remarkable journey. An area you nurture blossoms into a meaningful path for your social life, connecting you with others on a similar trajectory, willing to support your world with thoughtful discussions and opportunities to mingle. Sharing with valued companions promotes well-being and happiness.

13 Sunday

When Saturn turns retrograde, it invites you to reflect on your responsibilities, commitments, and long-term goals. It is a time for introspection and review, where you can assess the structures and limitations in your life. You may need to reassess your priorities and make necessary adjustments to align with your true purpose and inner wisdom. With the Moon entering Pisces, your emotions may become more sensitive and intuitive.

14 Monday

Focusing intensely on your goals provides a solid foundation for meaningful growth. This concentration aligns perfectly with the opportunities that surround you. From this broader vantage point, you unlock possibilities to nurture and enhance your innate talents. Embracing change on the horizon boosts skills and stimulates growth. It's time to take a dedicated approach to new endeavors, sharing your gifts with a larger audience and attracting rising prospects.

15 Tuesday

You seize an enterprising chapter marked by engagement and activity. The fruitful outcome on the horizon enables you to blaze a trail toward rising prospects, promising a time of prosperity that draws advancement and growth pathways. Working with your talents bears fruit and illuminates a journey that refines your skills. A new vision unfolds as the path shimmers with golden opportunities, ushering in a pivotal time for advancing and developing areas of interest.

16 Wednesday

When the Moon enters Aries, you may experience a surge of energy and a renewed passion and enthusiasm. This fiery and assertive energy encourages you to take the initiative and embrace new beginnings. It's a time to be bold, confident, and decisive in pursuing your goals and desires. You might be more assertive in expressing your needs and standing up for yourself. Embrace the spirit of adventure and embrace the opportunities that come your way.

17 Thursday

Releasing stress and anxiety enables you to move forward and break fresh ground. It helps you renew and rejuvenate your spirit as opportunities come knocking, bringing a boost into your world. Reawakening your sense of adventure opens a rich landscape of possibility. This time amplifies intuition, and you can trust your instincts to guide you to make the right decision. As you broaden the scope of what is possible, you harness creativity to achieve growth.

18 Friday

When Mercury turns retrograde, you may experience a period of introspection. Take the opportunity to slow down and reassess ideas and decisions. The Moon's ingress into Taurus brings a stabilizing influence, grounding you in practicality and a desire for comfort. This combination encourages you to approach challenges with patience and practicality. Additionally, the sextile between Mercury and Venus enhances your communication skills and social interactions.

19 Saturday

Exciting new energy surges into your world, ushering in change and initiating an expressive phase that offers renewal and rejuvenation. It opens the doors to a journey that brings social engagement and happiness. Sharing with kindred spirits sparks brainstorming sessions, providing opportunities for collaboration. This newfound motivation fuels expansion and taps into a creative vibe that cracks the code to rising prospects.

20 Sunday

When the Moon moves into Gemini, you may notice a shift in your emotional state and communication style. Your curiosity and intellectual curiosity heighten, encouraging you to engage in stimulating conversations and explore new ideas. It is a time for mental agility and adaptability, allowing you to embrace change and different perspectives. You may seek variety and diversity in your social interactions, craving mental stimulation and a sense of lightheartedness.

21 Monday

Creating room to nurture your talents initiates an optimistic shift, signifying a significant turning point in your journey. It propels you forward, fostering a fruitful atmosphere for growth and transformation giving you the freedom to explore creative expansion in novel domains. This period marks a positive influence, shaping a meaningful path forward. A broader theme of change and discovery envelops your life, fostering enriching conversations and inspiring ideas.

22 Tuesday

When the Moon moves into Cancer and the Sun enters Leo, you can explore the depths of your emotions and embrace your inner warmth and radiance. This time of heightened sensitivity and emotional connection allows you to nurture and care for yourself and others. You may seek comfort and security in the familiar. By aligning with your emotions and expressing yourself authentically, you can create a fulfilling and vibrant experience during this cosmic dance of Cancer and Leo.

23 Wednesday

With the Sun sextile Uranus, you may experience excitement and an urge to break from routine. This aspect sparks innovation and encourages you to embrace change and explore new possibilities. You can step out of your comfort zone and embrace your individuality. It's a time to express your unique style and showcase your creative ideas. However, the Venus square Mars aspect can bring a touch of tension in your relationships and desires.

24 Thursday

The Sun trine Saturn brings a harmonious alignment between your sense of self and your responsibilities and commitments. It's a time of stability and discipline, where you can steadily progress towards your goals. With the Moon ingress Leo, you infuse with confidence, creativity, and a desire to express yourself authentically. This combination encourages you to shine and take bold steps toward your aspirations.

25 Friday

When the Sun opposes Pluto, it brings to light dynamics and power struggles that may be playing out in your life. This aspect challenges you to confront and transform any patterns or situations hindering your growth. You may feel a sense of resistance or external pressures pushing you to question your sense of self and your power. Navigating this energy with awareness and integrity is essential, recognizing that true empowerment comes from within.

26 Saturday

When the Moon ingresses Virgo, you may be in a practical and analytical mindset. This energy encourages you to focus on details, organization, and productivity. You are motivated to improve efficiency and create a sense of order. It's a great time to tackle tasks, solve problems, and focus on minor aspects of your daily routine. Use this energy to be methodical and diligent while caring for your physical and emotional needs.

27 Sunday

The horizon hints at imminent changes, filling your heart with a sense of lightness and optimism as you anticipate new opportunities. Beautiful options infuse life with inspiring energy. A shift on the horizon introduces new companions into your life, breathing life into friendships. By being open to meeting new people, you tap into unique opportunities, fostering a social environment teeming with engagement and support, where lively moments with friends are the norm.

28 Monday

You link up with a happy chapter that opens to new opportunities. You turn a corner, which positions you to improve your life as you direct your energy into an area worth your time. It helps shake off the heavy vibes clinging to your power. News is coming, guiding the path forward, bringing a welcome distraction that nurtures creativity. Getting involved with growing your life helps you smooth out the bumpy patches as you head towards a bright chapter. It unlocks a time of growth and rising prospects.

29 Tuesday

When the Moon enters Libra, you may feel a heightened sense of harmony and a desire for balance. This transit focuses on relationships and social interactions, encouraging you to seek companionship and cooperation. You may find yourself drawn to beauty and aesthetics, appreciating art, music, and the finer things in life. It's an excellent time to engage in diplomatic conversations and seek compromise in conflicts.

30 Wednesday

A refreshing change of pace draws new possibilities into your social life. It helps you shut the door on a challenging chapter and reboots the potential possible in your world. An impromptu get-together with friends draws lively discussions. It brings a strong emphasis on improving the foundations of your life. You unpack a colorful chapter that brings new possibilities to light. A positive change on the horizon seals the deal on a refreshing landscape of opportunity.

31 Thursday

The Sun's conjunction with Mercury amplifies your mental focus and communication skills, making it a suitable time for clear and assertive expression. Use this powerful combination of energies to strengthen your connections with others through open-hearted conversations and compassionate understanding. Embrace the opportunity to deepen emotional intimacy and foster meaningful connections in your personal and professional relationships.

AUGUST

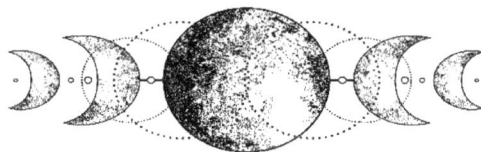

MOON MAGIC

Sun	Mon	Tue	Wed	Thu	Fri	Sat
					1	2
3	4	5	6	7	8	9
10	11	12	13	14	15	16
17	18	19	20	21	22	23
24	25	26	27	28	29	30
31						

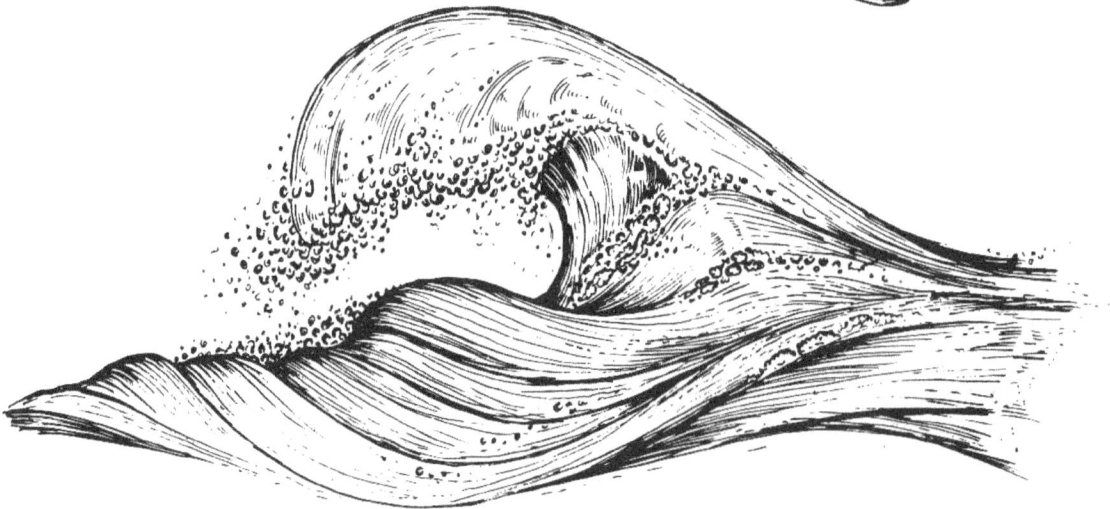

New Moon

STURGEON MOON

AUGUST

1 Friday

When Venus forms a square with Saturn and then later with Neptune, it can create some challenging emotional dynamics in your relationships. You may feel limited and restricted in expressing your affection and love. Connecting with others on a deep emotional level might be challenging, and there could be a sense of disappointment or disillusionment in your interactions. It's essential during this time to be patient with yourself and others, as miscommunications could arise.

2 Saturday

Significant changes highlight a journey of growth and progress. Attractive options usher in new possibilities, increasing motivation and infusing your life with a rekindled sense of lightness. This path takes you on an adventure that nurtures thoughtful discussions with kindred spirits, showcasing an environment marked by expressiveness and optimism that promotes companionship. It introduces a promising chapter in your social engagement, promising a delightful outcome.

3 Sunday

As the Moon ingresses into Sagittarius, you may feel more adventurous and optimistic. This cosmic shift brings a sense of enthusiasm and curiosity, encouraging you to explore ideas and broaden your horizons. You might desire freedom and independence during this time, seeking opportunities to expand your knowledge and experience different cultures or belief systems. Let the Moon's presence in Sagittarius guide exciting possibilities and meaningful growth.

4 Monday

Anticipate a shift in your life, as a new opportunity enables you to channel your energy productively and efficiently. You're headed toward growth with options that support your progression. A powerful influence encourages your creativity, cultivating a unique landscape filled with productivity and energy. This change heralds a period of significant transformation that will lead your life forward while an influx of social and career opportunities enrich your journey.

5 Tuesday

As the Moon enters Capricorn, you may feel more focused, disciplined, and determined. This transit brings a sense of practicality and a strong desire to achieve your goals. It's a great time to set clear intentions and work diligently towards making them a reality. The Capricorn influence encourages you to take charge of your life and responsibilities, reminding you of the importance of staying grounded and organized.

6 Wednesday

Mars ingress Libra. Embrace the spirit of cooperation and seek to create win-win situations in your interactions. While Mars in Libra may bring a desire for peace and cooperation, it also reminds you to assert your needs respectfully. Strive to maintain equilibrium in your actions and decisions, as this will lead to more positive outcomes in your personal and professional life. As Mars enters Libra, you may experience a shift in how you assert yourself and pursue your desires.

7 Thursday

Your life is set to light up with new potential, and by taking matters into your own hands, you yield fruitful results. A decisive period allows you to reach for your dreams proactively. A refreshing change of pace shatters old patterns and ways of thinking, setting you on a journey of new horizons, sparking movement and discovery. Growing and expanding your social and working life improves the foundations of stability in your world.

8 Friday

With the Moon entering Aquarius and Mars forming a trine with Uranus, you might feel excitement and a desire for novelty and adventure. You could be more open to trying new things and breaking free from old routines during this time. It's an excellent opportunity to explore individuality and embrace your unique qualities. You may feel a boost of energy and confidence, propelling you to take on new challenges and pursue innovative ideas.

9 Saturday

With Mars forming oppositions to Saturn and Neptune and the Full Moon illuminating the sky, you may feel a sense of tension and conflicting energies in your surroundings. Mars opposed Saturn can create a sense of frustration and limitations, making it feel like you're facing obstacles in your path. It leads to feelings of impatience and the need to assert yourself. However, the Full Moon's influence urges you to find balance and emotional release during this intensity.

10 Sunday

Moon ingress Pisces. Mars trine Pluto. With Mars trine Pluto, you can tap into your inner strength and make significant strides in areas that may have felt stagnant or challenging. It's a time to embrace transformation and channel your energy into activities that align with your passions and positively change your life. Trust your instincts and allow the cosmic energies to support you as you navigate this period of growth and self-discovery.

11 Monday

With Mercury turning direct, you may feel a sense of relief as communication and decision-making become more straightforward and less prone to misunderstandings. You might have experienced delays and technical glitches during retrograde, but now you can move forward with greater clarity and efficiency. It is an ideal time to revisit any stalled projects or unresolved issues and take action to resolve them.

12 Tuesday

With Saturn sextile Uranus, you may find that stability and innovation come into harmonious alignment. As the Moon enters Aries, you might feel a surge of energy and motivation, ready to take on new challenges and projects. Embrace this dynamic energy to initiate new endeavors and pursue your goals with confidence and enthusiasm. This astrological combination offers a fertile ground for positive transformations and opportunities, so seize the moment and make the most of it.

13 Wednesday

Fortune is ready to shine upon your life. It brings options that help you move towards an energizing chapter of social engagement. You can remove the doubt as you build a bridge towards a happier chapter. It enables you to expand your horizons as networking with friends introduces you to new companions worth your time. It brings lively discussions, and this wellspring of support in your broader social environment draws healing energy that nurtures your spirit.

14 Thursday

As the Moon enters Taurus, you may notice a shift in your emotional landscape towards a more grounded and stable state. This period offers an opportunity to focus on cultivating comfort and security. You may find yourself drawn to life's simple pleasures, seeking out moments of relaxation and indulgence. It's an ideal time to connect with nature, enjoy good food, and surround yourself with beauty and sensuality.

15 Friday

With Mercury sextile Mars, you may find that your communication skills are sharp and assertive. Your mind is quick and active, and you can confidently and enthusiastically express your thoughts and ideas. This aspect enhances your ability to make decisions and take action, as you have the mental agility to assess situations swiftly and effectively. It's an excellent time to engage in debates or negotiations, as your words carry impact and persuasiveness.

16 Saturday

With the Moon ingress Gemini, you might experience a shift in your emotional landscape, embracing a more curious and communicative mood. You may crave mental stimulation, seeking engaging conversations and exploring various topics. It is when your thoughts and emotions may fluctuate rapidly, like the ever-changing winds of Gemini. Embrace this versatility and adaptability, allowing yourself to learn and grow through new experiences and connections.

17 Sunday

A social aspect lights the way forward and sees you progress towards a supportive environment. It offers a thoughtful exploration path as sharing your ideas with others draws harmony to your surroundings. Focusing on developing ties draws grounded foundations, which become a rock-solid basis for expanding life outwardly. Many newnesses are coming into your world, helping you turn a corner and head towards gold.

18 Monday

Mercury forms a harmonious sextile with Mars, so your communication and thought processes become infused with dynamic energy and assertiveness. This alignment encourages you to express your ideas with clarity and passion, making it an opportune time to engage in persuasive conversations or tackle intellectually challenging tasks. Meanwhile, the Moon's ingress into Cancer deepens your emotional sensitivity and strengthens your sense of nurturing and intuition.

19 Tuesday

New options arrive soon, which brings a lift into your life. It lets you transition to a happy phase where you see improvement and progress. A clear path opens to guide you towards rising prospects—an area you nurture and develop picks up speed, bringing your dreams into focus. Being open to new possibilities becomes the gateway from which you grow your world. Your life picks up the pace, and forward momentum carries you towards an extended time of advancing goals.

20 Wednesday

As the Moon moves into the sign of Leo, you may feel more vibrant and expressive today. Your emotions infuse with a theatrical flair, and you'll likely seek attention and appreciation from those around you. This lunar influence can boost your confidence and creative energy, inspiring you to engage in activities that bring joy and excitement. You may feel a stronger desire to lead and take center stage, embracing your natural charisma and charm.

21 Thursday

Improvement ahead cracks the code to building stable foundations in your life. It brings a winning chapter that draws many blessings into your world. An influence emerging helps you develop some dreams you've had on the back burner. Getting involved in progressing your vision forward illustrates a sunny aspect that brings inspiration into your life. News arrives that brings a boost and leaves you feeling excited about the potential around your life.

22 Friday

As the Sun moves into Virgo, you may feel a shift in your focus and approach to life. This astrological event brings a time of practicality, attention to detail, and a desire for efficiency in your daily activities. Your analytical abilities heighten, making identifying and implementing organized systems to enhance your life easier. You may be drawn to self-improvement and health-oriented activities to establish a more balanced and disciplined routine.

23 Saturday

Moon ingress Virgo. New Moon. This period encourages you to prioritize self-care and wellness, making it an ideal time to adopt healthier habits and routines. Allow the New Moon's energy to inspire you to let go of what no longer serves you and make room for growth and positive changes in your life. Use this potent lunar phase to align your actions with your intentions and embark on a personal development and success journey.

24 Sunday

Sun square Uranus. Embrace the opportunity for personal growth and innovation that this aspect offers. Be open to exploring new ideas and perspectives, even if they initially seem unconventional. Finding creative solutions to challenges can lead to exciting breakthroughs and a deeper understanding of yourself. Remember to stay grounded amidst the fluctuations and trust your ability to adapt and thrive in this dynamic period.

25 Monday

The Moon in Libra brings a desire for balance and harmony in your relationships, encouraging you to seek compromise and understanding with others. Your diplomatic approach and appreciation for beauty can enhance your connections and bring peace. With Venus in Leo, your romantic and creative side takes center stage, and you may find yourself drawn to express love and affection more boldly and passionately.

26 Tuesday

Venus trine Saturn. Venus sextile Uranus. Venus trine Neptune. This combination of aspects creates a beautifully balanced and inspiring atmosphere for love, creativity, and emotional fulfillment, where you can cherish the familiar's stability and embrace the magic of the unexpected. It's a time to savor the richness of your connections and explore new dimensions of intimacy and shared experiences with those you hold dear.

27 Wednesday

As Venus opposes Pluto, you may encounter intense emotions and power dynamics in your relationships and interactions. This astrological aspect can bring forth feelings of possessiveness, jealousy, and a need for control, which might lead to conflicts or power struggles. Be mindful of hidden agendas or manipulative tendencies within yourself and others, as they could disrupt the harmony and trust in your connections.

28 Thursday

Moon ingress Scorpio. This lunar transit brings intensity and passion to your experiences, making you more attuned to the hidden layers of emotions within yourself and others. You may seek more meaningful connections and crave authenticity in your interactions. It is a time to embrace your inner strength and resilience, as Scorpio's influence encourages you to confront any emotional challenges with courage and determination.

29 Friday

Uranus sextile Neptune. During this time, your imagination may soar, and you may feel more attuned to the subtle energies and mysteries of the universe. Embrace Uranus's transformative power and Neptune's ethereal influence to tap into your higher consciousness and channel your unique vision into creative projects or spiritual practices. This aspect encourages you to trust your instincts and embrace the unknown, which can lead to significant personal growth.

30 Saturday

The Moon, in Sagittarius, brings a sense of adventure and a longing for exploration, both in the external world and within your inner realms. You might strongly desire to break free from routine and seek new experiences that broaden your horizons. This lunar transit encourages you to embrace a more open-minded and adventurous approach to life, allowing yourself to step out of your comfort zone and pursue your dreams with a renewed sense of purpose.

31 Sunday

Opportunities ahead create greater ease in your life. It does bring a grounded foundation that enables stability to emerge. Life takes on a meandering pace as you comfortably explore new leads. Indeed, slowing down brings a focus on improving circumstances, which draws rejuvenation and renewal. It offers beautiful changes that give you a more relaxed and happy environment. Taking time to relax helps bring ease and flow back into your life.

SEPTEMBER

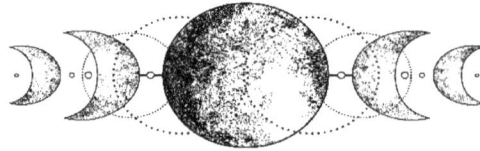

MOON MAGIC

Sun	Mon	Tue	Wed	Thu	Fri	Sat
	1	2	3	4	5	6
7	8	9	10	11	12	13
14	15	16	17	18	19	20
21	22	23	24	25	26	27
28	29	30				

NEW MOON

CORN/HARVEST MOON

SEPTEMBER

1 Monday

Saturn ingress Pisces influence brings sensitivity and compassion to your journey, prompting you to become more attuned to your emotions and those of others. During this period, you may find it beneficial to explore spiritual practices or engage in creative and imaginative pursuits that help you connect with your inner self on a profound level. Saturn's presence in Pisces encourages you to embrace empathy and intuition as you navigate life's challenges and responsibilities.

2 Tuesday

As the Moon moves into Capricorn and Mercury enters Virgo, you may experience a period of increased focus on practicality and productivity. The Moon in Capricorn brings a sense of discipline and a desire for tangible achievements, motivating you to set clear goals and work diligently. With Mercury in Virgo, your communication style becomes more precise and detail-oriented, allowing you to analyze information critically and articulate your thoughts effectively.

3 Wednesday

Mercury square Uranus. The square aspect can create tension between the desire for independence and stability in your thoughts and communication. Embrace the unique perspectives that Uranus brings, but also take the time to ground yourself and consider the potential consequences of your actions and words. With mindfulness, you can harness the electric energy of this square to spark creative solutions, leading to fresh breakthroughs and personal growth.

4 Thursday

Moon ingress Aquarius. Your emotions may focus more on community and social causes, inspiring you to connect with like-minded individuals and contribute to collective endeavors. This transit is a favorable time to engage in intellectual discussions and explore innovative ideas. Embrace the Aquarian energy to celebrate your authenticity and use your emotions to catalyze positive change in your life and the world.

5 Friday

Mars square Jupiter. While this square aspect can bring adventure and daring to your actions, temper it with practicality and foresight to maximize its positive impact and avoid unnecessary setbacks. Embrace the courage and drive this alignment provides, and exercise mindful decision-making to make the most of this dynamic planetary configuration. You can enjoy this vibrant energy and achieve meaningful progress by being conscious of your actions and decisions.

6 Saturday

As Uranus turns retrograde, you might experience a subtle shift in your external circumstances and inner reflections. During this period, you may revisit past experiences or reconsider your approach to personal growth and individuality. Uranus' retrograde motion encourages you to look inward and question the areas of your life where you seek greater independence and freedom. This aspect is an opportune time to break free from limiting beliefs holding you back.

7 Sunday

The Full Moon lunar phase marks a time of increased illumination and clarity, where intentions set during the New Moon come to fruition. It's a period of heightened awareness and emotional intensity, and you might find yourself reflecting on past events and gaining valuable insights. Full Moons often highlight the need for balance between opposing forces, so pay attention to areas where you feel a tug-of-war between different aspects of your life.

8 Monday

Moon ingress Aries. It's a time to trust your instincts and embrace a more courageous approach to life. During this phase, you may need personal freedom and self-expression, inspiring you to follow your passions and embrace new beginnings. Harness the dynamic energy of the Aries Moon to step out of your comfort zone, explore new possibilities, and confidently assert your individuality. It brings an original journey that feels the right fit for your life.

9 Tuesday

A helpful avenue opens that brings a busy time. Gathering your resources and planning for future growth lets you create the stepping stones that take you toward success. A new opportunity gives you the green light to link with development and progress. It offers a cutting-edge initiative that refines your skills and amplifies your abilities. Actively tapping into the potential around your creativity attracts a new assignment worth your time.

10 Wednesday

Moon ingress Taurus. Taurus' influence brings a sense of calm and serenity, encouraging you to find comfort and security in life's simple pleasures. During this lunar transit, you may feel a stronger connection to nature and desire sensory experiences. Taurus is associated with appreciating beauty and the arts, so you might find yourself drawn to activities that engage your senses, such as enjoying good food, soothing music, or spending time in nature.

11 Thursday

Working with your creativity attracts a breakthrough that places you in alignment to develop your skills. You are on the cusp of change; it marks a time that expands your horizons outwardly. It sees you gliding forward as you capture the essence of inspiration and begin building your dreams. A fortunate trend arrives that takes your vision to a new level. It gives you the green light to merge creativity with tangible results.

12 Friday

Sun sextile Jupiter's astrological aspect can bring a surge of confidence and opportunities for growth and success. As the Moon moves into Gemini, your emotional landscape becomes more curious and adaptable. You might find yourself drawn to social interactions and engaging in lively conversations. Mercury also forming a sextile to Jupiter enhances your communication skills, and you can express your ideas with enthusiasm and clarity.

13 Saturday

Sun conjunct Mercury. Your ability to absorb information is enhanced, making learning and problem-solving more accessible. Embrace this conjunction's energy to engage in meaningful conversations, express yourself authentically, and gain valuable insights into aspects of your life. It's a time of intellectual prowess and heightened self-awareness, so make the most of it by utilizing your mental acuity to pursue your goals and foster harmonious connections with those around you.

14 Sunday

Significant changes on the horizon highlight a journey of growth and progress. Attractive options usher in new possibilities, increasing motivation and infusing life with a rekindled lightness. This path takes you on an adventure that nurtures thoughtful discussions with kindred spirits, showcasing an environment marked by expressiveness and optimism that promotes companionship. It introduces a promising chapter in your social engagement, promising a delightful outcome.

15 Monday

As the Moon enters Cancer, you may notice a shift in your emotions, becoming more attuned to your inner feelings and the needs of others. Cancer's influence brings a nurturing and compassionate energy, encouraging you to seek comfort and security in familiar and close relationships. During this lunar transit, you may feel a stronger connection to your home and family, finding solace in the warmth of your domestic surroundings.

16 Tuesday

Venus sextile Mars. You exude a magnetic charm that draws others to you, and your ability to express your feelings with grace and confidence heightens. Use this harmonious energy to explore your desires and find ways to create a fulfilling balance between your emotional and physical needs. Embrace the opportunities the Venus-Mars sextile presents to strengthen your bonds with others and infuse your life with a healthy dose of love and excitement.

17 Wednesday

As the Moon moves into Leo, you may feel a surge of confidence and desire for self-expression. This lunar transit enhances your creativity and charisma, urging you to enter the spotlight and share your unique talents with the world. However, with Mercury opposed to Saturn, you might also encounter challenges in your communication and decision-making. Your thoughts could feel restricted or hindered by self-doubt or external limitations.

18 Thursday

Mercury ingress Libra. Mercury opposed Neptune. Use Libra Mercury's influence to foster open and honest communication, seeking clarity in your discussions with others. Embrace the art of compromise and active listening to navigate any potential challenges the Mercury-Neptune opposition may present. With careful consideration, you can use this energy to bring about greater understanding and meaningful connections in your interactions.

19 Friday

As Mercury forms harmonious trines to Uranus and Pluto, you may experience a period of intellectual breakthroughs and profound insights. These astrological alignments enhance your mental agility and intuition, making it an excellent time for problem-solving and uncovering hidden truths. Your thoughts are sharp, and you may discover innovative ideas and unconventional approaches. Your creative and visionary thoughts allow you to grasp complex concepts quickly.

20 Saturday

Venus Square Uranus' astrological influence can bring a sense of restlessness and a need for excitement in your romantic life. It's essential to be open to exploring new possibilities and cautious of impulsive actions leading to instability or conflicts. Embrace the transformative energy of Venus square Uranus as a chance to break free from old patterns and embrace your individuality, allowing for more authentic and fulfilling connections in your emotional landscape.

21 Sunday

With the Sun opposed to Saturn, you may encounter inner tension and external challenges that test your determination. This astrological aspect can restrict or delay your plans, leading to frustration or self-doubt. However, with the New Moon and the Moon's ingress into Libra, there's an opportunity for a fresh start and balance. This lunar phase encourages you to set new intentions and focus on finding harmony in your relationships and decision-making processes.

22 Monday

Mars ingress Scorpio. September Equinox. Sun ingress Libra. It is an excellent time for fostering diplomacy and cooperation, as Libra's influence encourages you to consider different perspectives and strive for balance. Embrace the powerful and transformative energy of Mars in Scorpio, along with the significance of the September Equinox and the harmonious qualities of the Sun in Libra, to embark on a journey of self-discovery and growth, fostering more profound connections.

23 Tuesday

When the Sun opposes Neptune, you may experience confusion and uncertainty in various aspects of your life. This astrological aspect can bring a sense of vagueness or idealism, making it difficult to see things clearly or make concrete decisions. You might daydream or escape reality, leading to a lack of focus and direction. It's essential to be cautious of potential deception or self-deception during this time, as it challenges your judgment.

24 Wednesday

With the Sun forming harmonious trines to Uranus and Pluto, you may experience a powerful surge of transformative energy and newfound confidence. This astrological alignment inspires you to embrace change and take bold, innovative steps toward your goals. The trine to Uranus sparks a sense of independence and a desire for liberation, motivating you to break free from old patterns and embrace your uniqueness.

25 Thursday

You soon find stable foundations that ground your spirit in a new area of interest. Re-evaluating the path ahead helps you ascertain the right way forward. Revelations appear, enriching your life experience and unveiling a rich tapestry of meaningful goals. This transformation becomes a turning point, ushering in an era of advancement in various aspects of your life, including a surge in creativity under sunny skies. New options promise a rewarding journey of exploration.

26 Friday

Moon ingress Sagittarius lunar transit fosters a desire for exploration and a thirst for knowledge. You might seek new experiences and broaden your perspectives. The Sagittarius Moon encourages you to embrace a positive outlook on life and to be open to different cultures and belief systems. During this time, you may feel a greater need for freedom and independence, valuing your autonomy and the opportunity to embark on new physical or intellectual journeys.

27 Saturday

Being open to change draws new possibilities into your life. It does expand horizons and bring an exciting time when you can grow and improve your daily life. Rejuvenation and renewal nurture well-being in your life as you get involved with sharing and caring for friends. Mixing with your tribe reduces stress and supports a journey of healing and discovery. Something special is brewing in the background, creating a potent mix of potential in your life.

28 Sunday

You enter a more stable phase that brings a passageway toward a brighter future. It lets you release any restrictive patterns and advance towards more critical goals in your life. Opening the book to a new chapter brings a gateway forward. It nurtures your creativity and helps you build something substantial in your life. It teams you up with others who match your interests as you draw movement and discovery into your world.

OCTOBER

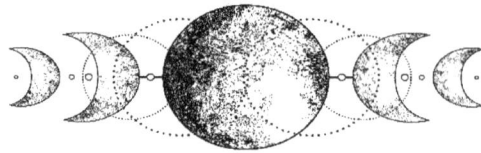

MOON MAGIC

Sun	Mon	Tue	Wed	Thu	Fri	Sat
			1	2	3	4
5	6	7	8	9	10	11
12	13	14	15	16	17	18
19	20	21	22	23	24	25
26	27	28	29	30	31	

New Moon

HUNTERS MOON

29 Monday

As the Moon enters Capricorn, you may notice a shift towards a more disciplined and practical emotional state. This astrological influence encourages you to focus on your long-term goals and take a structured approach to your feelings. Your emotions become more reserved, urging you to prioritize responsibility and productivity. Capricorn's energy fosters a sense of determination and ambition, making it an ideal time to set intentions and work diligently toward aspirations.

30 Tuesday

Looking at where blocks in your life limit progress can help lift the shutters on a purpose-driven chapter. An innovative approach takes you on a path that develops your abilities and refines your skills. It brings learning, research, and development, helping you create the type of stability that nurtures security around your life. Exploring new options for your working life brings pathways that lead you toward growth. It brings a role on offer that lights up avenues of prosperity.

1 Wednesday

As the Moon enters Aquarius, you might experience a shift towards a more open-minded and innovative emotional state. This astrological transit encourages you to embrace your uniqueness and connect with others in a more socially conscious and progressive way. However, Mercury square Jupiter has a potential for information overload or exaggerated thinking. It's essential to exercise caution in your communication and avoid making decisions based on over-optimistic views.

2 Thursday

As you make notable tracks on improving your situation, you discover a positive momentum that carries you forward. It brings surprises, invitations, and news into your world. An upward trend marks an expressive time for engaging with your friends. It brings a memorable time of lightness and harmony that lets you touch down on a journey that speaks to your spirit. It offers a prosperous time for sharing thoughts and discussing possibilities with friends.

3 Friday

Lovely changes ahead come a great way to grow your life. It brings a trailblazing journey that offers a whirlwind of activity in your social life. It connects you with unique characters who add zest to your life. Mingling with friends brings expansion and growth into focus. Blossoming potential swirls around the periphery of your situation but grows into a valid path forward. Riding a wave of hopeful energy, you shift your focus to exploring the possibilities with friends.

4 Saturday

Moon ingress Pisces. You may find solace in serene environments or engaging in activities that nourish your soul. During this lunar transition, your empathy and compassion towards others may become more pronounced, leading to a desire to help and support those in need. Embrace the Pisces Moon's energy to dive into your emotions, seek inspiration from your dreams, and connect with the depths of your imagination for a period of healing, renewal, and emotional connection.

5 Sunday

As you dabble in new interests, you embark on growing your world. New options crop up to inspire a sense of wanderlust. Reawakening creativity brings growth and happiness. Your pioneering spirit lets you turn the corner and connect with expansion, adventure, and excitement. You soon hit your stride in a journey that grows your life in a unique direction. Listening to the call of the wild within your spirit heightens confidence and brings motivation to continue growing life.

6 Monday

Mercury ingress Scorpio. You might draw research or investigation during this lunar transit. The Aries Moon's energy encourages you to trust your instincts and take the lead in initiating actions that align with your emotions. Embrace the Mercury in Scorpio influence to dig beneath the surface and engage in deep and meaningful conversations. Use this time to proactively address your feelings and pursue intellectual endeavors that resonate with your passions.

7 Tuesday

During a Full Moon, you may experience heightened emotions and a sense of culmination. This astrological phase illuminates what is hiding, bringing emotions and situations to their peak. However, with Mercury square Pluto, there might be challenges in communication and potential power struggles. This aspect can lead to intense conversations where emotions and opinions run deep. It's essential to be cautious of manipulation and confrontations during this time.

8 Wednesday

Venus sextile Jupiter alignment enhances your social interactions, making it an excellent time for engaging in activities that bring you happiness. The combination of the Taurus Moon and Venus sextile Jupiter encourages you to embrace the richness of your experiences, from enjoying delicious food to spending quality time with loved ones. Use this transit to foster a harmonious balance between material and emotional well-being with warmth and abundance.

9 Thursday

Exploring new leads for your working life draws a pleasing result. It brings a shift forward that provides you with new inspiration. It brings possibilities that help you blaze a trail forward toward a secure destination. New job possibilities link you with a chapter that offers a clear direction for your working life. Inspiration and excitement rise to meet the opportunities that flow into your world. A colorful chapter ahead draws happiness into your world.

10 Friday

As the Moon moves into Gemini, you may notice a shift towards curiosity and communication. This astrological influence encourages you to engage in lively conversations and seek mental stimulation. Gemini's energy fosters a desire to learn and explore various topics, making it an ideal time to connect with others. Your emotions become more adaptable and changeable, allowing you to shift between different perspectives and engage in light-hearted interactions.

11 Saturday

With Venus opposed to Saturn, you may encounter emotional challenges and limitations in your relationships. Use this period for self-reflection and growth, addressing any underlying issues inhibiting the flow of affection and connection. While this aspect can bring some difficulties, it also offers an opportunity for personal development, allowing you to work on building healthier relationships and fostering a more balanced and resilient approach to matters of the heart.

12 Sunday

As the Moon moves into Cancer, you may experience heightened emotional sensitivity and a desire for comfort and security. This astrological shift encourages you to connect with your feelings deeper and seek solace in familiar environments. Cancer's energy fosters a nurturing and compassionate atmosphere, making it an ideal time to spend quality moments with loved ones and engage in self-care practices that nourish your soul.

13 Monday

As Venus moves into Libra, you may experience a shift towards a greater emphasis on harmony, relationships, and aesthetic appreciation. This astrological influence encourages you to seek balance and beauty in your interactions with others. Libra's energy fosters a sense of diplomacy and a desire for fairness, making it an excellent time to collaborate. You might seek artistic pursuits or social activities that allow you to connect with others on a deeper level.

14 Tuesday

With Venus opposed to Neptune, you may experience a period of romantic idealism and potential confusion in matters of the heart. This astrological aspect encourages you to approach relationships and desires cautiously, as illusions and unrealistic expectations might cloud your judgment. However, as Pluto turns direct, you're entering a phase of transformation and empowerment. This shift can prompt you to confront deep-seated issues and positively change your life.

15 Wednesday

Being open to new possibilities uncovers pathways that take you toward growth, bringing a passageway toward a brighter future. It helps you step out into an environment filled with blossoming activities, with a remarkable change ahead offering room to grow your life. An emphasis on improving your foundations sees circumstances shift and head towards rising prospects, unwrapping a time of endless possibilities, engaging activities, and expansion.

16 Thursday

With the Moon moving into Virgo, you may notice a shift towards a more analytical and practical emotional state. This astrological transition encourages you to focus on details, organization, and efficiency. Virgo's energy fosters a desire for order and precision in your surroundings and tasks. During this lunar transit, you might find satisfaction in taking care of practical responsibilities and addressing any issues that require attention.

17 Friday

Sun square Jupiter's astrological aspect can bring a sense of optimism and confidence. Still, avoiding overestimating your capabilities or taking on more than you can handle is essential. There's a possibility of being overly extravagant or overlooking crucial details due to inflated enthusiasm. While this aspect can encourage growth and expansion, balancing ambition and practicality is essential. Embrace the Jupiter-inspired positivity, but channel it into achievable goals.

18 Saturday

Your well-crafted ideas soon get a chance to be developed. It brings a busy time that nurtures growth in your life as you break free of limitations and cultivate many possibilities. It offers a stimulating environment as you mingle with friends. Light-hearted discussions see creativity blossoming. As you ride a wave of hopeful energy, your life enjoys a sunny aspect that helps you chart a course toward an upward trend. Building stable foundations in your life nourishes your life.

19 Sunday

As the Moon moves into Libra, you may notice a shift towards seeking harmony and balance in your emotions and interactions. This astrological transition encourages you to prioritize fairness and cooperation, valuing relationships and social connections. Libra's energy fosters a desire for beauty and aesthetics, making it an excellent time to engage in creative activities or surround yourself with pleasing surroundings.

20 Monday

With Mercury conjunct with Mars, you may experience heightened mental activity and assertiveness. This astrological alignment enhances your ability to confidently and passionately express your thoughts and ideas. Your mind becomes more focused and sharp, allowing you to tackle tasks and challenges head-on. This conjunction can inspire you to assertively communicate your desires and intentions, but being mindful of others in your interactions is essential.

21 Tuesday

During a New Moon, you have the opportunity to set new intentions. This astrological phase marks the start of a new lunar cycle, inviting you to plant seeds of growth and transformation. As the Moon moves into Scorpio, your emotions become more intense and introspective. Scorpio's energy encourages you to delve into deeper emotional realms and uncover hidden truths. It is a time for embracing change and renewal, shedding old layers, and embracing your inner strength.

22 Wednesday

As Neptune moves into Pisces, this astrological transition encourages you to tap into your intuitive and imaginative faculties, fostering a deeper connection to your inner world and the subtle energies around you. Pisces' energy aligns well with Neptune's influence, creating a harmonious atmosphere for introspection, creativity, and compassion. During this period, you might crave artistic pursuits, meditation, and exploring mystical or esoteric subjects.

23 Thursday

Sun ingress Scorpio's astrological transition encourages you to embrace the mysteries of life and explore the realms of emotions, passion, and transformation. Scorpio's energy fosters a sense of intensity and a willingness to confront your fears and desires with courage and determination. This period invites you to shed light on the concealed, allowing for personal growth and the opportunity to release what no longer serves you.

24 Friday

With the Moon moving into Sagittarius, you might experience a sense of adventurous enthusiasm and a desire for exploration. This astrological influence encourages you to expand your horizons and seek new experiences. However, the Sun's square to Pluto adds intensity to the atmosphere. This aspect can bring about power struggles and potential for internal transformation as you confront hidden parts of yourself.

25 Saturday

When Mercury forms a trine aspect to Saturn, you may experience a period of increased mental discipline and focused communication. This astrological alignment enhances your ability to think logically and strategically, making it a favorable time for planning, organizing, and tackling tasks that require attention to detail. Your thoughts become more structured and practical, allowing you to make sound decisions and communicate clearly and precisely.

26 Sunday

As the Moon moves into Capricorn, you may notice a shift towards a more focused and disciplined emotional state. This astrological transition encourages you to approach your feelings with practicality and a sense of responsibility. Capricorn's energy fosters a desire for accomplishment and a willingness to work hard towards your goals. During this lunar transition, you might find satisfaction in setting and achieving tasks that contribute to your long-term aspirations.

27 Monday

Adjusting to new circumstances is never easy, but creating a stable foundation enables you to move forward in a balanced manner. It brings sound energy that sees life evolving and becoming more prosperous, positioning you to develop a journey that nurtures an abundant landscape as you touch down on a new chapter of possibility for your life, with further options sparking your interest, marking a turning point that lets you head towards growth and prosperity.

28 Tuesday

With Mars forming a trine to Jupiter, you may experience amplified energy and an increased drive for achievement. This astrological alignment enhances your motivation and enthusiasm, making it an ideal time to pursue your goals confidently. Your actions become more purposeful and expansive, and you might find yourself taking on new challenges with a positive attitude. This trine encourages you to take calculated risks and seize growth opportunities.

29 Wednesday

As Mercury enters Sagittarius, your thinking becomes more expansive and open-minded, encouraging you to explore new horizons and seek knowledge. The Mars trine Saturn adds a sense of disciplined determination, allowing you to pursue your goals with practicality and perseverance. However, the Mercury-opposed Uranus could introduce unexpected twists in your thinking and conversations, prompting you to adapt to new and sometimes unconventional ideas.

30 Thursday

Mercury sextile Pluto astrological alignment empowers you to uncover hidden truths beneath the surface. Your thoughts become more focused, allowing you to engage in conversations that have a profound impact. This sextile encourages you to embrace your analytical and investigative skills, making it an excellent time for research, problem-solving, and exploring complex topics. Use Mercury-Pluto sextile's energy to engage in discussions and tap into your intellectual prowess.

NOVEMBER

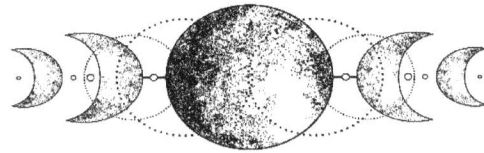

MOON MAGIC

Sun	Mon	Tue	Wed	Thu	Fri	Sat
						1
2	3	4	5	6	7	8
9	10	11	12	13	14	15
16	17	18	19	20	21	22
23	24	25	26	27	28	29
30						

NEW MOON

BEAVER MOON

31 Friday

Moon ingress Pisces astrological transition encourages you to connect with your inner world and explore your feelings more deeply. Pisces' energy fosters a sense of compassion and empathy, making it a favorable time to engage in acts of kindness and support for others. During this lunar transit, you might find solace in creative activities or spiritual practices that allow you to tap into your imagination and connect with the intangible.

1 Saturday

A new influence arrives in your life. It grounds your energy in a productive journey forward. Life becomes more accessible, expansive, and involved. It sees inspiration flowing into your world, restoring faith in the path ahead. It drives a social and comprehensive chapter of connecting with friends. News arrives that brings an invitation to mingle. A door opens, which brings communication into your world. It helps you embrace a more socially active environment.

2 Sunday

Moon ingress Aries astrological shift encourages you to take initiative and enthusiastically pursue your desires. Aries' energy fosters a sense of independence and a willingness to embrace new challenges. However, with Venus squaring Jupiter, there's a potential for indulgence and excess in matters of the heart and pleasure. This aspect can bring forth a desire for extravagance or overestimate the potential outcomes of your actions.

3 Monday

Unexpected news ahead brings an open road of possibility into your life, working with your abilities to attract an engaging and happy journey, your willingness to stay open to new possibilities drawing a pleasing result and a shift forward that grows your world in a unique direction, discovering an option that feels like a good fit for your life, entering a refreshing time to stay in sync with your vision for growth, a busy time of developing goals as you enjoy a whirlwind of activity.

4 Tuesday

As Mars forms a trine to Neptune, you may experience inspired action and heightened intuition. This astrological alignment empowers you to pursue your goals with imagination and determination. With Mars moving into Sagittarius, your actions become infused with adventurous and expansive energy. As the Moon moves into Taurus, your emotions may seek stability and comfort, drawing you towards sensual pleasures and a desire for security.

5 Wednesday

Full Moon offers an opportunity to reflect on goals and intentions set during the New Moon phase and to make adjustments—time to release what no longer serves and to celebrate achievements. Embrace the energy of the Full Moon to gain insight into your emotions, acknowledge your progress, and find a balance between your desires and practical realities. Use this decisive cosmic moment to embrace the revelations of this lunar peak.

6 Thursday

Mars sextile Pluto astrological alignment encourages you to tackle challenges strategically. As the Moon moves into Gemini, your emotions become more adaptable and communicative. Simultaneously, with Venus entering Scorpio, your approach to relationships and matters of the heart takes on a more intense and passionate quality. This combination of influences encourages you to express your desires openly and engage in meaningful conversations.

7 Friday

Information arrives for you soon, sparking your attention. Indeed, you are wise to stay open to new possibilities as this adds spice and flavor to your world, triggering a social aspect that brings bright and cheerful energy your way. Sharing lively and entertaining conversations gets a boost, paving the way toward expanding horizons. You attract the right opportunities into your world. Life stirs up exciting endeavors that spark growth in your world.

8 Saturday

The Uranus-Taurus influence invites you to find new and unconventional ways to approach your resources. At the same time, the Venus-Pluto square encourages you to confront emotional dynamics and empower yourself in your connections. Embrace the Cancer Moon's energy to seek comfort in your close relationships and navigate this transformative period with adaptability, emotional awareness, and the courage to embrace new ideas.

9 Sunday

As Mercury turns retrograde, you may notice a shift in communication and information flow. This astrological phenomenon encourages you to slow down and take a closer look at your plans and interactions. During this period, misunderstandings and technical glitches could be more prevalent, prompting you to exercise caution when making important decisions. Mercury retrograde often encourages revision, urging you to revisit old projects or reassess your thoughts.

10 Monday

With the Moon moving into Leo, you may notice a shift toward a more expressive and confident emotional state. This astrological transition encourages you to embrace your inner radiance and shine your light. Leo's energy fosters a desire for recognition and a willingness to share your creativity and passions with others. During this lunar transit, you might find yourself seeking out activities that bring you joy and allow you to express yourself authentically.

11 Tuesday

As Jupiter turns retrograde, you may enter a period of introspection and reflection on your growth and expansion. This astrological shift encourages you to review your beliefs, aspirations, and long-term goals. While Jupiter's retrograde can slow the momentum of external progress, it offers an opportunity to delve into inner exploration. This cosmic phase is a time to reassess your plans and consider whether they align with your authentic values.

12 Wednesday

Mercury conjunct Mars. Moon ingress Virgo. This combination encourages you to combine your mental agility with a practical approach, allowing you to tackle tasks and address any issues that arise efficiently. Embrace the Mercury-Mars conjunction's energy to be proactive in your conversations and endeavors while using the Virgo Moon's influence to harness your attention to detail and organizational skills to navigate this dynamic and productive period.

13 Thursday

You're about to open the doors to a new chapter that fills you with optimism and a lighter spirit about the possibilities in your world. A social and lively environment reveals a journey filled with opportunities and connections that resonate with your outlook on life. Something significant is on the horizon, encouraging you to leap into a grand adventure that expands your horizons. You'll find a creative phase that nurtures your talents, stirring the pot of possibilities.

14 Friday

A change ahead brings a turning point, linking you with a social environment that adds an exciting flavor to your life. Mingling and networking bring positive communication and conversations, with ideas flowing as possibilities abound, making life lighter and bringing laughter and renewal to your door. Expanding your horizons brings you in contact with inspiring people who nurture happiness in your life.

15 Saturday

As the Moon moves into Libra, you may notice a shift towards a more harmonious and diplomatic emotional state. This astrological transition encourages you to seek balance and fairness in your interactions with others. Libra's energy fosters a desire for companionship and a willingness to compromise to create harmonious connections. During this lunar transition, you might attract activities promoting cooperation and understanding.

16 Sunday

If you feel adrift, you can use your abilities to bring goodness to the surface of your world, being open to growing your life as you transition towards heightened opportunities. It shifts your mindset towards an abundant focus, which improves your circumstances, and a remarkable change ahead offers room to grow your life, emphasizing the improvement of your foundations, seeing circumstances shift and head towards rising prospects.

17 Monday

With the Sun forming trines to Jupiter and Saturn, you may experience a balance between expansion and practicality. This astrological alignment empowers you with optimism and discipline, creating a harmonious synergy between your aspirations and your ability to manifest them. As Mercury sextiles Pluto, your communication becomes more transformative. As the Moon moves into Scorpio, your emotions deepen, urging exploration of the layers beneath the surface.

18 Tuesday

Sifting and sorting options help you spot an opportunity that has been flying under the radar, shifting you forward and enjoying a much-appreciated taste of freedom and excitement, expanding horizons to open up pathways that feel like a good fit for your restless energy. Jotting down plans and working towards your goals brings rejuvenation and a chance to rebrand your skills in an exciting area worth your time.

19 Wednesday

With Mercury moving into Scorpio, you may experience intensified and probing communication. This astrological shift encourages you to delve deep into matters and discover hidden truths. However, the Mercury-opposed Uranus aspect can bring about unexpected disruptions in your thoughts and conversations, potentially leading to sudden insights or changes of perspective. Mercury then forms a trine to Neptune; your thinking becomes more intuitive and imaginative.

20 Thursday

During a New Moon, you may find yourself at the beginning of a fresh cycle of intentions and possibilities. This astrological phase marks a time of planting seeds for future growth and setting preferences for the weeks ahead. As the Sun conjuncts Mercury, your thoughts and communication align with your core sense of self. With Mercury moving into Sagittarius, your thinking becomes more expansive and open to new perspectives.

21 Friday

As the Sun opposes Uranus, you may experience a period of unexpected disruptions and a desire for change. This astrological aspect can bring about a sense of restlessness and a need to break free from routine. It's a time to embrace innovation and consider unconventional paths. Simultaneously, the Sun trine Neptune adds a touch of dreaminess and imagination to your experiences. This transit encourages you to tap into your intuition and engage in creative pursuits.

22 Saturday

Embrace the Sagittarius Sun's energy to pursue your passions. This astrological transition encourages you to embrace new horizons and explore different perspectives while using the Mercury-Saturn trine to ensure practicality in your plans. Allow the Capricorn Moon to guide you in grounding your emotions and channeling your efforts towards tangible achievements, as the Mercury Jupiter trine supports your pursuit of knowledge and success during this dynamic period.

23 Sunday

Sun sextile Pluto astrological alignment encourages you to tap into your inner strength and make positive changes. The Sun's energy aligns with Pluto's regenerative and transformative qualities, allowing you to shed light on hidden aspects of your circumstances. This sextile empowers you to take charge and initiate changes that align with your personal growth. It invites you into deeper layers of your psyche, face hidden truths, and let go of what no longer serves you.

24 Monday

A currency of information flows into your life, giving you news and options to help you make an informed decision. It begins a journey that eclipses the past by opening your life to new experiences. It touches all areas of your life as it earmarks remarkable opportunities for growth ahead. It helps you forge new friendships and expand your life outwardly. Working towards your dreams offers tangible results that promote advancement in your life.

25 Tuesday

Mercury conjunct Venus. Moon ingress Aquarius. This combination encourages you to connect with others uniquely and open-mindedly, fostering a sense of community and cooperation. Embrace the Mercury-Venus conjunction's energy to engage in meaningful conversations while allowing the Aquarius Moon's influence to guide a more inclusive and forward-thinking approach to your interactions. Use this cosmic synergy to embrace the spirit of collective growth.

26 Wednesday

With Venus forming trines to Jupiter and Saturn, you may experience a balanced and harmonious energy in matters of love, relationships, and personal values. This astrological alignment empowers you with a sense of abundance and stability. The Venus Jupiter trine encourages the expansion of your heart, fostering a spirit of generosity and enjoyment of life's pleasures. The Venus-Saturn trine adds a practical and grounded influence, helping you establish solid foundations.

27 Thursday

As the Moon moves into Pisces on Thanksgiving, you may be more compassionate and reflective. This astrological transition encourages you to tap into your empathy and connect with the holiday's more profound, more emotional aspects. Pisces' energy fosters a sense of unity and a desire to express gratitude not only for the material aspects of life but also for the intangible gifts of love, compassion, and spirituality.

28 Friday

As Saturn turns direct, you may sense a shift in the cosmic energy around you. This astrological event signifies when Saturn, the planet of discipline, starts moving forward again. During this transition, you might feel a sense of clarity and forward momentum in areas related to responsibility, career, and personal growth. Saturn's direct motion encourages you to take the lessons and introspection of its retrograde phase and apply them to your plans and ambitions.

29 Saturday

As Mercury turns direct, you may feel a sense of relief and clarity in your communication and thought processes. This astrological event signifies the end of potential misunderstandings, delays, and technical glitches often accompanying Mercury retrograde. With Mercury moving forward, you can expect smoother conversations, more straightforward decision-making, and improved information flow.

30 Sunday

As Venus enters Sagittarius, your approach to love and pleasure becomes more adventurous and open-minded. Embrace the Aries Moon's energy to boldly pursue your desires while allowing the Venus-Uranus opposition to inspire you to navigate changes gracefully. The Venus-Neptune trine invites you to approach your relationships and creative endeavors with empathy and idealism as you embark on this period of passionate and expansive emotional experiences.

DECEMBER

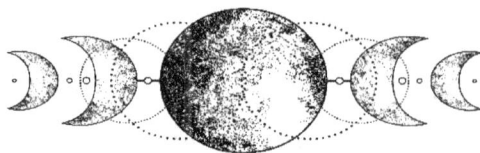

MOON MAGIC

Sun	Mon	Tue	Wed	Thu	Fri	Sat
	1	2	3	4	5	6
7	8	9	10	11	12	13
14	15	16	17	18	19	20
21	22	23	24	25	26	27
28	29	30	31			

New Moon

COLD MOON

December

1 Monday

Unique opportunities are incoming, bringing magic into your world, offering a pivotal time for rising prospects, and drawing new possibilities into your life. It lets you set up growth as you spot an area for development that holds water, highlighting growth and expansion in your life that promotes a positive trend. Working with your creativity magnifies the potential possible as you transition towards a fresh start.

2 Tuesday

With the Moon moving into Taurus, you may notice a shift towards a more grounded and stable emotional state. This astrological transition encourages you to seek comfort, security, and indulgence in simple pleasures. Taurus' energy fosters a sense of appreciation for the material world and a desire for stability. At the same time, the Venus sextile Pluto aspect adds depth and intensity to your relationships and passions.

3 Wednesday

A bright, breezy wind of refreshing potential puts a lighter influence into your sails. You are likely to be busy for the next few weeks, especially with communication as news arrives, triggering a social atmosphere that will make you feel a sense of belonging by connecting with friends, boosting the areas of your life that are currently quiet, finding a way to channel your energy into positive outlets that will bring a pleasing result, nurturing a happy time in your life.

4 Thursday

Embrace the Full Moon's energy to assess your progress and release what no longer serves you, all while harnessing the communicative prowess of Gemini to express your emotions and intentions. This phase invites you to find a balance between your rational mind and emotional heart as you navigate this period of heightened mental stimulation and the culmination of intentions set during the previous New Moon.

5 Friday

Engaging with a broader world of potential sees companionship flourish as new ideas and possibilities crop up, meeting progressive individuals who help you step into a different landscape, bringing a motivational time of investing energy into your social life, where lively discussions ensure bright ideas get new projects and endeavors to the surface. This positive influence fuels your creativity, and sharing ideas charts an auspicious journey toward fresh possibilities.

6 Saturday

As the Moon moves into Cancer, you may notice a shift towards a more nurturing and emotionally sensitive state. This astrological transition encourages you to prioritize your emotional well-being and seek comfort in familiar surroundings. Cancer's energy fosters a deep connection to your feelings and an inclination to care for yourself and others. Additionally, with Mercury forming a trine with Neptune, your communication takes on an intuitive and compassionate quality.

7 Sunday

Focusing on social engagement opens a path of connection and companionship, bringing a positive influence that helps you grow a meaningful journey forward, introducing a more comprehensive theme of change and expansion into your life. Socializing and networking lead to a lovely get-together with like-minded people who boost morale and share ideas, creating a spontaneous and lively environment for you to enjoy.

8 Monday

Life is ripe with potential and ready to blossom, offering choices and decisions that promote rapid expansion as you shift your focus toward developing your career path. Mapping out long-term goals becomes a turning point, enabling you to chase your vision and gain traction on improving circumstances, using your talents to stunning effect as you head towards change, a time that offers opportunities for growth and expansion.

9 Tuesday

Mars square Saturn's astrological aspect can clash between your desires for action and the limitations or responsibilities Saturn represents. You might find that your efforts are met with resistance or delays, which can be frustrating. However, this aspect also offers an opportunity for discipline and patience. It encourages you to assess your goals and plans, ensuring they align with your long-term objectives. You can navigate this cosmic challenge and emerge better prepared for success.

10 Wednesday

With the Moon moving into Virgo, you may notice a shift towards a more practical and detail-oriented emotional state. This astrological transition encourages you to focus on organization and efficiency in your daily life. Virgo's energy fosters a desire for order and a keen eye for perfectionism. Simultaneously, Neptune's change in direction from retrograde to direct can bring clarity and inspiration to your dreams and intuition.

11 Thursday

Mercury trine Neptune. Mercury ingress Sagittarius. This combination fosters a favorable environment for exploring different cultures and belief systems. Embrace the Mercury-Neptune trine's energy to express your thoughts compassionately and connect with others on a deeper, more empathetic level. Allow the Mercury in Sagittarius influence to inspire your intellectual pursuits and adventurous spirit as you navigate with creativity, wisdom, and curiosity.

12 Friday

Moon ingress Libra. During this lunar transit, you might crave social activities and engage in conversations that create understanding and unity. Your sense of aesthetics may also be heightened, inspiring you to appreciate beauty in your surroundings and perhaps engage in creative pursuits. Embrace the Libra Moon's energy to foster meaningful connections, create an atmosphere of grace, and seek out the shared values that bring people together in a spirit of mutual respect.

13 Saturday

With Mercury forming a sextile to Pluto, you may find that your thoughts and communication take on a more insightful quality. This astrological aspect encourages you to uncover hidden truths beneath the surface. It's a favorable time for researching, problem-solving, and engaging in conversations that have a profound impact. You might notice an increased ability to focus your mind on complex subjects and get to the heart of matters with precision.

14 Sunday

Mars square Neptune. It's crucial during this time to be cautious about making impulsive decisions, as your judgment might be impaired. Embrace the Mars-Neptune square as a signal to take a step back, reevaluate your plans, and be mindful of potential hidden obstacles or motivations. It's a time to practice patience and ensure that you clearly understand your intentions and the reality of your situation before taking action.

15 Monday

You may feel an intense emotional shift as the Moon moves into Scorpio. This astrological transition encourages you to explore your innermost feelings and confront any underlying issues with determination. Scorpio's energy fosters a desire for transformation and a willingness to dive into the depths of your emotions. Additionally, with Mars moving into Capricorn, you'll likely experience a surge of discipline and ambition in your actions and pursuits.

16 Tuesday

As you delve deeper into your future goals, you unearth a treasure trove of possibilities that keeps the fires of potential burning. This discovery unlocks a pathway of growth and rising prospects, smoothing out any bumps on your path to advancement. Life becomes more accessible, expansive, and engaged, and nurturing your talents fuels this growth, enabling you to climb the ladder to a successful outcome—upcoming news ushers in a forward-facing environment.

17 Wednesday

With the Sun forming a square to Saturn, you might encounter a sense of limitation. This astrological aspect can bring challenges and obstacles to the forefront, making it feel like you're facing resistance in your pursuits. Being patient and persistent during this time is essential, as your ambitions may be met with delays or setbacks. However, as the Moon moves into Sagittarius, you'll feel a shift towards a more optimistic and adventurous emotional state.

18 Thursday

Life heads towards an upward trend, opening a gateway that brings a journey of new adventures, adding a spontaneous element that attracts clear skies overhead. Invitations crop up that feel like a good fit for your social life, kicking the cobwebs to the curb and enjoying sharing with your broader circle of friends. Networking and mingling promote new ideas and possibilities for future development. It creates space to nurture new goals as positive energy flows into your world.

19 Friday

News ahead brings new potential into your life. It attracts a time that offers many blessings for your social life. Laughter, fun, and increasing social engagement provide a relaxed environment that nurtures well-being and happiness. It shines a light on rejuvenation as you turn the corner and enter a more dynamic chapter. Balancing stability promotes a social landscape that creates possibilities for friendship and collaboration. It lets you drift toward a happier and lighter time.

20 Saturday

With the Black Moon entering Sagittarius, you may feel a pull towards expanding your horizons and seeking new experiences and knowledge. Embrace the New Moon's energy to set clear intentions as it marks a time of planting seeds, utilize the Capricorn Moon's practicality to take tangible steps towards your goals, and let the Black Moon in Sagittarius inspire you to explore uncharted territories on your journey of growth and self-discovery.

21 Sunday

With the Sun forming a square to Neptune, uncertainty might cloud your vision. This astrological aspect can bring about moments of doubt and vulnerability, making it essential to exercise caution in decision-making and to be mindful of potential illusions or misunderstandings. Simultaneously, Venus squares Saturn, which could introduce a feeling of restriction or distance in your relationships and financial matters.

22 Monday

With the Moon's transition into Aquarius, you might feel a shift towards a more intellectually inclined and socially aware emotional state. This astrological movement encourages you to embrace your individuality and a sense of open-mindedness. Aquarius' energy fosters a desire to connect with like-minded individuals who share your passions and ideals. It's an excellent time to engage in group activities, seek unique experiences, and explore unconventional ideas.

23 Tuesday

New options arrive, which bring a lovely change to your environment. It supports growth, expansion, and greater social involvement. Being open to growing in your life in a unique direction helps you overcome the barriers that impede progress. As the path ahead clears, it brings an open road of new adventures. Designing your life becomes a focus that emphasizes the development of new possibilities. It draws an environment that is soul-affirming and enriching.

24 Wednesday

Venus square Neptune's astrological aspect can bring about a sense of idealism and a desire for romantic or artistic experiences that may not align with reality. It's essential to exercise caution in relationships and financial matters during this time, as the Neptune influence may obscure clear judgment. As Venus moves into Capricorn, you're entering a period emphasizing a more practical and disciplined approach to your values and relationships.

25 Thursday

As the Moon moves into Pisces on Christmas Day, you will likely experience a profoundly emotional and compassionate atmosphere. This astrological transition encourages you to embrace the season's spirit with empathy and an open heart. Pisces' energy fosters a sense of unity and a desire to connect with the emotions and needs of others. It's a beautiful time to express love and kindness to those around you and to immerse yourself in the joy of giving.

26 Friday

Life keeps the fires of motivation burning as you mingle with kindred spirits and achieve expansion in your social life. It brings a connected time that offers pathways for networking. Joint projects with other kindred spirits help grow and advance your abilities. It brings your work to a broader audience, leading to exciting possibilities. It marks a brighter, lighter time and dynamically connects with people who promote kinship and connection.

27 Saturday

As the Moon charges into Aries, you might sense a surge of dynamic energy and a desire for action. This astrological shift encourages you to embrace assertiveness and take initiative. Aries' energy fosters a pioneering spirit, motivating you to tackle challenges head-on and make bold decisions. You might find yourself drawn to new beginnings and adventures during this time, eager to start fresh and pursue your passions with enthusiasm.

28 Sunday

As you dig deeper into your future goals and aspirations, you discover insight into the path ahead. It helps you unleash your abilities into an exciting area that tips the scales in your favor. A tried-and-true formula sees you using a planning strategy to come out on top. It positions you in an environment that grows your life outwardly. It helps you break fresh ground, bringing the sunshine blooming overhead.

29 Monday

As the Moon gracefully enters Taurus, you may notice a shift to a more grounded and stable emotional state. This astrological transition encourages you to seek comfort, security, and a connection to the physical world. Taurus' energy fosters a desire for simplicity, indulgence in life's pleasures, and a sense of appreciation for the material aspects of life. During this time, you might find solace in enjoying good food, embracing creature comforts, or spending time in nature.

30 Tuesday

When Mercury squares Saturn, you may face communication challenges and mental hurdles. Your thoughts and ideas may clash with the practical, disciplined approach Saturn encourages. It can feel like your mind is weighed down by self-doubt and a sense of limitation, making it difficult to express yourself confidently. This aspect can lead to a tendency to overthink or be overly critical of your words and actions.

31 Wednesday

Moon ingress Gemini lunar shift can infuse your celebrations with light-hearted and communicative energy, making it an ideal time for connecting with friends and loved ones. You might engage in lively conversations, share stories, and embrace a more adaptable and curious mindset. It's an opportunity to ring in the new year with intellectual curiosity and playfulness as you seek new experiences and connections that keep the festivities vibrant and engaging.

1 Thursday

On New Year's Day, Mercury ingresses into Capricorn and forms a challenging square aspect with Neptune; you might encounter mental fog and confusion that contrasts with the usual clarity you seek when setting New Year's resolutions and goals. Your thought processes could become clouded, making it challenging to express your intentions precisely, as Neptune's influence may lead you to perceive situations through a more dreamy lens.

Astrology, Tarot & Horoscope Books.

Mystic Cat

Mystic Cat Tarot

In Relationship Reading
$15.00

Crossroads
$10.00

Next Relationship Reading
$15.00

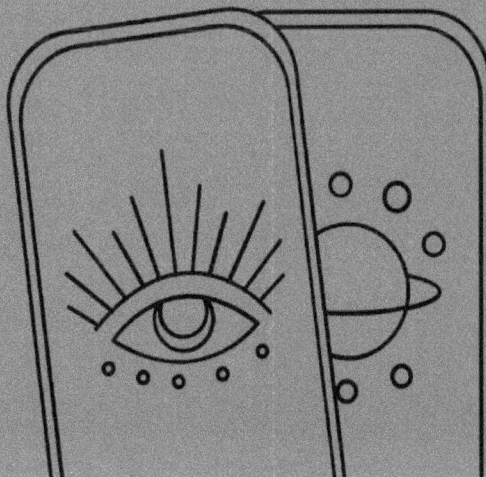

Ohoroscope@Hotmail.com

www.ingramcontent.com/pod-product-compliance
Lightning Source LLC
Chambersburg PA
CBHW080530090426
42733CB00015B/2541